**Revd Phyllis Thompson** is a member of the leadership team at the New Testament Church of God, Northampton, having served as Education Director for NTCG from 2007 to 2018. An EQUIP certified trainer, she is a member of NTCG's International Division of Education Board and an Executive Council member of the European Pentecostal Theological Association. She is the editor of *Challenges of Black Pentecostal Leadership in the 21st Century* (SPCK, 2013).

'I had the honour of delivering the inaugural lecture for the first series of the Oliver Lyseight lectures that focused on Pentecostal leadership. That was more than a decade ago, and I want to commend the vision and tenacity of Phyllis Thompson, editor, for concluding a second series of these lectures on Pentecostal theology with this important work. This volume continues in pursuit of the original aim: to improve the ministry of the Pentecostal Church which, in spite of inherent dynamism and Spirit-driven growth, has needed the buttress of a maturing theology – particularly one developed by its own scholars and practitioners. The themes discussed in this volume contribute to the continuing development of this youthful ecclesial movement, a mere century old within a two-millennia-old Christian Church, on its way to greater theological and missional effectiveness. As one inducted into faith and shaped by Pentecostalism, I warmly welcome and commend this important work.'

**Joe Aldred**, Honorary Research Fellow, Roehampton University, Bishop in the Church of God of Prophecy and Principal Officer for Pentecostal & Charismatic Relations, Churches Together in England

'We have here insightful reflections on Pentecostal theology and its methods in the light of changing Christian and societal landscapes. With particular focus on black and minority ethnic groups, and the rejection they have faced, the book calls for responsible theology and godly living to go hand in hand – at individual, communal and even political levels – all enabled by personal encounter with God's Holy Spirit.'

**William P. Atkinson**, Chair, European Pentecostal Theological Association and Senior Lecturer, London School of Theology

'When we consider that one in four Christians is a Pentecostal, this book is a must for all who are seeking to improve their knowledge of Pentecostal theology and recognize its distinctives. I wholeheartedly recommend this book to preachers, teachers, students and Christians of all persuasions. It offers a range of perspectives from which to address some of the current challenges facing Pentecostal

theology. It also enables us to identify opportunities to apply some practical solutions in the interest of Pentecostalism and its contribution to the wider Christian witness in the twenty-first century.'
**Donald Bolt**, Administrative Bishop, New Testament Church of God England and Wales

'Here is a selection of voices addressing "pertinent Pentecostal predicaments" that are longstanding and current – including spirituality, theology, modernity, money and politics. It is a must-read book for present-day and emerging Pentecostal scholars as they engage with the challenges and examine them further.'
**Dulcie Dixon McKenzie**, Director of the Centre for Black Theology, Queen's Foundation, Birmingham

'That Pentecostalism is a formidable contributor to Christian witness is a reality. We are, however, living in unprecedented times, and there are many challenges to this Pentecostal witness. The series of lectures which gave rise to this book has given us the opportunity to self-interrogate Pentecostalism and its contribution in the twenty-first century: What is the core of this tradition? How truly effective is Pentecostalism in equipping its leadership and members for discipleship today? This is not simply a book for Pentecostals by Pentecostals. It is a helpful resource for anyone who wishes to engage with Pentecostalism. It offers not only a grown-up assessment of the essence of Pentecostalism but also the real scrutiny that is needed to ensure a Pentecostalism that is fit for purpose.'
**Rose Hudson-Wilkin MBE, QHC**, Bishop of Dover

'The multi-faceted chapters of this book broaden, deepen and affirm our understanding of Pentecostalism as a living way of expressing the Christian faith in today's world. There is passion and information here, advice for the present and hope for the future.'
**William K. Kay**, Honorary Fellow, Institute for Pentecostal Theology, Regents Theological College

# CHALLENGES OF PENTECOSTAL THEOLOGY IN THE 21ST CENTURY

Edited by
Phyllis Thompson

First published in Great Britain in 2020

Society for Promoting Christian Knowledge
36 Causton Street
London SW1P 4ST
www.spck.org.uk

*British Library Cataloguing-in-Publication Data*
A catalogue record for this book is available from the British Library

ISBN 978–0–281–08425–8
eBook ISBN 978–0–281–08426–5

Typeset by Fakenham Prepress Solutions, Fakenham, Norfolk NR21 8NL

eBook by Fakenham Prepress Solutions, Fakenham, Norfolk NR21 8NL

To the pioneers of the New Testament Church of God in the UK: those who served at the forefront and those who served behind the scenes.

# Contents

# Contributors

**Revd Dr Joel Edwards** is a writer, coach, Bible teacher and international inspirational speaker, covering issues of social justice, leadership, faith and society. In 2019, he was awarded a DThM from St John's College, Durham, where he is also a visiting fellow. Joel's wide range of experience includes 10 years as a local pastor in the East End of London, more than 15 years as a freelance broadcaster with the BBC, 11 years as General Director of the Evangelical Alliance UK and 10 years' leadership in Micah Challenge International – a global faith-based response to extreme poverty. He has also served as advisor to the Foreign Secretary's Advisory Group on Human Rights, as well as a commissioner on the UK Equalities and Human Rights Commission.

**Charlotte V. V. Johnson** is a human resources professional working in the public sector and an executive trustee of a charity for people with learning disabilities. She is currently pursuing a Doctor of Ministry qualification through the New Testament Church of God Leadership Training Centre in partnership with the Pentecostal Theological Seminary in Cleveland, USA.

**Revd Dr Steven Land** is a minister of the Church of God and a member of the Pentecostal Theological Seminary faculty in Cleveland, USA, where he developed courses on the Theology of Holiness, the Theology of Wesley, Divine Healing, Pentecostal Foundations for Theological Study and Ministry, Apologetics, and Pentecostal Spirituality-Theology. He is a founding editor of the international *Journal of Pentecostal Theology* and is the author of *Pentecostal Spirituality: A passion for the kingdom* (CPT Press, 2010).

## List of contributors

**Revd Dr Douglas Nelson** has served as an ordained minister of the United Methodist Church, USA. He earned his doctorate from the University of Birmingham, UK, with a dissertation entitled 'For Such a Time as This: The story of Bishop Williams J. Seymour and the Azusa Street Revival'.

**Revd Dr Keith Warrington** is Emeritus Reader in New Testament and Pentecostal Studies at Regents Theological College, West Malvern, UK. He also directs Word and Spirit, a programme that enables believers to engage with the Bible in ways that are transformative (<www.wordandspirit.info>). His recent books include *The Miracles in the Gospels* (SPCK, 2015) and, co-edited with Trevor Burke, *A Biblical Theology of the Holy Spirit* (SPCK, 2014).

# Acknowledgements

I am indebted to Sue Howard and Lynn Vickery for the time and effort they gave to read and share their observations in order to help my completion of the introduction and conclusion to this series of lectures.

Sincere thanks to Sharon Constance, who laboured on the typescript, and Eustace Constance who kept us going with his creative cuisine, and to both of them for their gracious willingness to proofread the manuscript.

I also want to thank Michael Bolt, Nastassia Holness and Sadie Lindsey-Brooks for their administration of this series of lectures.

Credit is due to the five lecturers for their acceptance of our invitation to deliver the lectures and then to reproduce them for publication. Gratitude is extended to Dr David Sang-Ehil Han for editing the lecture delivered by Revd Dr Steven Land.

In one way or another the following people have informed my theological perspective and I am delighted that they have taken the time to read and endorse this compilation: Revd Dr Joe Aldred, Revd Dr William Atkinson, Bishop Donald Bolt, Dr Dulcie Dixon, Bishop Rose Hudson-Wilkin and Professor William Kay.

Thanks are due to everyone who attended the lectures and made them such a rich learning experience with their contribution of questions and observations. I am aware that the conversations and learning continue beyond the events and for that I am greatly gratified.

I would also like to thank SPCK, especially Philip Law, the publishing director, who saw the potential of this volume and welcomed our submission.

# Introduction

PHYLLIS THOMPSON

The Oliver Lyseight annual lectures are an attempt by the New Testament Church of God to facilitate conversations among ourselves and in the company of others to improve our ministry and fulfil our kingdom purposes. We will have achieved a measure of success if this series of lectures stirs up willingness among Pentecostal church leaders, and black majority Pentecostal leaders in the UK in particular, to seize opportunities to explore our Pentecostal theological heritage in greater depth, and to lead our congregations into a theological maturity that enables a strong sense of identity and confidence to address the challenges of the twenty-first century.

The five lectures delivered between 2013 and 2017 follow an earlier series of five to commemorate the life and ministry of Bishop Dr Oliver Lyseight, the founding father of the New Testament Church of God in England and Wales. The series aims to identify and explore some of the present-day issues and pertinent challenges facing Pentecostal theology. What are its distinctive features? How does it inform our hermeneutics? Does Pentecostal theology reinforce our nonconformist legacy? How does this brand of theology speak to global conundrums such as racial injustice? Does it inadvertently accommodate the Prosperity Gospel? What resources can we draw on to sustain Pentecostal identity and nurture adherents for a better future?

Theology gives shape and meaning to our spiritual experience. It provides a structural base for people to process and develop their knowledge and understanding, as well as to enhance their confidence of and in the faith. The following narrative presents a typical Pentecostal testimony and, as such, provides a good point of reference for the five chapters in this publication:

> My parents and pastors taught me that my relationship with God included salvation, water baptism, sanctification, and baptism in the Spirit. These were experiences that every believer needed and should desire. Growing up in the church, there were countless occasions when I responded to an altar call for salvation, healing, strength, and all God does at a Pentecostal altar . . . Although I began to preach at age 15, it was not until I was 20 that the Lord baptized me in the Spirit . . . A few months after my Pentecostal experience, the State Overseer approached me and said, 'I want you to go to Coachella, California, to take your ministerial exam.' I had never been to Coachella, much less aspired to take an exam for credentials within the Church of God. However, that Spring of 1985, I realized this was God's plan for my life. It has been through the empowerment of the Spirit that I have sustained a ministerial journey of almost 35 years.[1]

# The quest for Pentecostal theology – a theology of encounter

Pentecostalism, as we know it today, is indeed a young member of the Christian family. As Keith Warrington observes in the first chapter, it is just over a hundred years old and still in the process of growth and development, expressing itself in a variety of forms and styles, and in a range of cultural and global contexts.

Keith Warrington poses some pertinent questions. What is it that makes a Pentecostal? He mentions two key indicative theological traits: the Christ-centred emphasis on Christ as saviour, healer, sanctifier, baptizer in the spirit and soon-coming King, and the belief in baptism in the Spirit and speaking in tongues as the initial evidence. Warrington makes the point that these distinctions have become blurred as 'most Pentecostal beliefs are also [now] accepted by millions of Charismatic believers' and are thus becoming less exclusive to Pentecostalism. At the same time, some former characteristics are becoming contested within Pentecostalism itself.

Whereas some Pentecostals, particularly those with Wesleyan roots, hold strongly to the five-fold composition of the Christ-centred dogma and seek to make it tangible in their lives and ministry, there are those who struggle to do so. Drawing on my own experience as a Pentecostal minister and educator, I believe that, to some extent, the struggle follows insubstantial coaching in Christian discipleship and is manifested in confusion about what it means to be 'saved'. Some adherents struggle through lack of theological clarity; for example, the concept of 'knowing Christ as Sanctifier' is not fully grasped, so it remains an abstract declaration or statement of belief with little understanding of its application to life. For some, the struggle is due to incongruence between their lived experience and their biblical knowledge; for example, what are Pentecostal members taught to understand about sickness and healing, and death for that matter? How is that understanding taught? And how, if at all, is Pentecostal eschatology presented? For example, does our preaching and teaching heighten or diminish expectations about the return of Christ?

Speaking in tongues as an initial or key sign of baptism in the Spirit has been questioned by some Pentecostals in recent times. Notwithstanding the debate, and in answer to some of the questions he poses, Warrington offers useful pastoral wisdom in words that inspire spiritual imagination. For him, Pentecostalism is to do with the theology of encounter: 'a personal, experiential encounter of the Spirit of God'. He visualizes and describes the 'heartbeat' of Pentecostal spirituality as an expectation of possibilities offered by the Spirit for 'a journey of discovery, a quest for a destiny, an exploration of the inexplicable that will touch and transform . . . lives.' This position, however, raises questions about individualism, subjectivity, sensitivity, the need to preserve balance and accountability. In fact, one may ask, who sanctions the very notion of a Pentecostal spirituality?

As well as challenges to do with the authenticity of the orientation of the individual within the movement, there is also wavering consent about the legitimacy of tongue-speaking as the initial evidence of the 'encounter with Spirit'. Warrington expresses his concern about the impact of this prerequisite and, quoting Poloma, argues that 'we face a major challenge . . . [in that] . . . "In some Classical Pentecostal circles, glossolalia is in danger of becoming a doctrine devoid of experience".'[2]

Drawing on William Kay's thoughts about the three levels of Pentecostal theology, one opportunity to address this challenge might be the promotion of interchanges between the theology of (a) the Pentecostal congregation, based on their personal Bible reading, the sermon of the local pastor and their religious experience; (b) the Pentecostal ministers, who may or may not have received a seminary education; and (c) the Pentecostal academic community.[3] A pertinent matter of concern when the challenges of Pentecostal theology are being discussed is whether the 'personal encounter' is sufficient for Pentecostal ministers or whether theological education, training and continuing ministerial development should be mandatory additional expectations.

The sharing of experience and insights or revelation under the scrutiny of others is wise (Proverbs 11.14; 15.22; 24.6). What if, in the interest of their own learning, all Pentecostal leaders made it their duty to engage with other Pentecostals beyond their denomination as well as with broader ecumenical groups?

Warrington exhorts us to 'learn from our tradition', train those we lead to 'listen' to the Spirit and seize opportunities to

'teach others to do the same' in order to sustain our distinctiveness and make our Pentecostal contribution to the Christian
voice in the twenty-first century.

# Pentecostal theology in our postmodern world

Douglas Nelson invites us to consider some of the prevailing
methodologies used to critique the Bible which challenge the
reverential view held by Pentecostals of its unadulterated truth-
fulness, and our devotional approach to reading and applying
its truth to our daily life. From this perspective, his opening
quotation positively positions Pentecostalism in the wider
scheme:

> God hath chosen the foolish things of the world to confound
> the wise; and God hath chosen the weak things of the world
> to confound the things which are mighty; And base things of
> the world, and things which are despised, hath God chosen,
> yea, and things which are not, to bring to nought things that
> are: That no flesh should glory in his presence.
> (1 Corinthians 1.27–29)

Nelson uses the ministry of William Seymour to substantiate
his line of reasoning. He accredits the term 'Pentecostal movement' to Seymour and relates 'Pentecostal spirituality', as it
emerged from the Azusa Street events, to the exemplary depth
of Seymour's level of spirituality, theological base and pastoral
leadership. In Nelson's considered opinion, although Seymour
'led the greatest Christian revival of the twentieth century, arguably the greatest of all time . . . [he is often] forgotten, a prophet
without honour . . . because of the racial separations that followed . . . when . . . the white Christians departed from their

black brothers and sisters . . .' Herein lies the conundrum we live with when we use the terms black majority churches and black caucuses, or refer to white majority denominations or historic churches, black and minority ethnic groups, black ministries or multicultural ministries. What these labels represent, and how they do justice to our reading of Galatians 3.28–29 when related to racial inequalities, and to John 13.34–35 in relation to unconditional love, is problematic. This, of course, raises major questions for Pentecostals about how far we replicate the values and mindset of society, how we challenge world views that are incompatible with our brand of theology, and what added value our Pentecostal exegesis and hermeneutics bring to Christian spirituality in the here and now of our global village. On the issue of racial injustice experienced as prejudice or separation within the Pentecostal family, Nelson boldly asserts that 'This sinful separation has never been admitted as wrong, or confessed by the white separatists.' To this day, as it is commonly noted, on Sunday mornings, we get a picture of the global Church in its most segregated semblance, and the Pentecostal family continues to contribute to this jigsaw.

Nelson's imaginative contemplation of the story of Simon of Cyrene brings colour, emotion, sound and meaning to the narrative of the cross in a typical Pentecostal style. Furthermore, it places Simon, the black leader, in a prominent position which is, more often than not, overlooked in our ministry of the Word in preaching, teaching and other modes of delivery, such as the arts.

If postmodernism means the denial of absolute truth in preference to relative truths, how does the theology gained from what is heard and learned by those in the pews, those in the pulpits and those in the academic communities counteract so-called 'relative truths', and inform as well as inspire Pentecostals to live what is believed? Nelson presents a strong case for a greater link between theology and practice in our lives as Pentecostals. Like all theologies, Pentecostal theology plays a critical role in the spiritual formation of its adherents, a point not to be taken lightly by those who present themselves as leaders, and too often as 'leaders' without any responsible lines of accountability.

This chapter alludes to links between black theology, liberation theology and Pentecostal theology. Questions about the contribution that black Pentecostals can offer to the Pentecostal movement to enrich the Christian voice and witness in the twenty-first century are brought to the fore: for example, to what extent are we equipped and positioned to draw on our experience of social exclusion and marginalization to nurture the current generation for a better future?

If Pentecostal theology is to be authentic, credible and sustainable in our world, it must be able to speak to all of God's creation and give voice to the interrelationship between the Godhead and creation. Black Pentecostals and black majority Pentecostal churches have a contribution to make to Pentecostal theology from our history and experience of exclusion and injustice. We have a responsibility to counteract the Eurocentric perspective that dominates Christian language, art and other expressions of the Christian faith. The artworks, for example, in many of our homes, churches and theological institutions portray the good news from the European's point of view. It hardly points to the vision we claim to share as presented in Revelation 7.9: 'After this I looked, and there before me was a great multitude that no one could count, from every nation, tribe and language, standing before the throne and before the lamb . . .' A critical question that faces us as a global family is 'What legacy are we leaving for the next generation?' We clearly have a lot to do.

# Pentecostalism and the Prosperity Gospel

The Prosperity Gospel poses another challenge to Pentecostals concerned about accurate interpretation of Scripture; in other words, a credible interpretation of Scripture that is harmonious with the experience of the individual and the doctrinal claims of the movement. Joel Edwards makes reference to the inadequacies of the 'sheltered subculture of Black classical Pentecostalism' in which many independent Pentecostal church groups of all ethnicities and cultural groupings can easily find themselves through lack of accountability processes and procedures. Personal experience and the interpretation of that experience are given precedence over the collective wisdom of the Pentecostal movement, as enshrined in its theological legacy.

An important legacy of Pentecostalism is the expectancy that a transformation will result from the change in values brought about by the ministry of the Holy Spirit in the life of the believer. As moral and ethical codes rooted in beliefs about holiness and righteousness are adopted and practised, the life of the adherent is improved; for example, the former drug addict or alcoholic becomes a respectable family member and responsible citizen. However, some disenfranchised Pentecostals have come to embrace the benefits gained from values and lifestyle choices they have learned to emulate within the movement; they inadvertently subscribe to a 'theology of empowerment' rather than the theology that grew out of the Holiness/Pentecostal experience. In Edwards' analysis, this presents a challenging 'dichotomy between spirit and matter, faith and finance'. Furthermore, he asserts, 'The horror is that it seeks to do so with a myopic ecclesiology and without a serious historical perspective.'

Holiness and integrity are fundamental to Pentecostalism. How these virtues are realized in our world of competitiveness, corruption in high places, austerity on a global scale and so on is a question rarely addressed in any depth in many of our local churches due to a lack of theological literacy. We are therefore in danger of fostering lifestyles rooted in assumptions rather than clearly considered theology. For example, we can become so consumed with our own quest for the 'blessed' life that we forget that we are 'blessed to be a blessing'.

Edwards reminds us of the purpose of sound theology and the unadulterated ministry of the Word. Historical theology is highlighted as a valid reference enabling us to ensure that the theology we profess points to the Godhead rather than to a charismatic personality or, in his words, an 'idolized personality' or 'self-appointed champion'.

The 'talk' is always easier than the 'walk'. Pentecostals, like all who claim to be Christians, are expected to exemplify moral responsibility in our private and public worlds if the theology we proclaim is to be respected. The Prosperity Gospel and its proponents have brought this matter into sharp focus, presenting the movement with a range of theological questions, concerns and apprehension.

In Edwards' observation, the variety of perspectives on the Prosperity Gospel around the world is not only demonstrative of the diverse theological positions within the movement but the challenge we have in defining and defending the non-negotiables of our Pentecostal theology.

With reference to the consultation on the Prosperity Gospel and the subsequent publication of Perriman's *Faith, Health and Prosperity*, Edwards provides an exemplary approach for how we might deal with differences we encounter with our brothers and sisters within our Christian family. We do not witness in isolation. We are part of the wider Church with accompanying responsibilities. The validity of ecumenical spaces and tables as opportunities for peer conversation, reflection and learning is well evidenced.

The chapter provides a potent case study which also challenges us to consider the extent to which our 'talk' and our 'walk' are in harmony, and present a theology that accentuates the mission of God, as opposed to our egocentric prospects. The chapter also exemplifies one way in which Pentecostals can make a contribution to the development of our own theology for our own good, and that of the wider Christian family and society at large.

## Pentecostalism: politics and justice

Steven Land echoes Edwards' observation in his opening statement: 'The global Pentecostal movement is rich and very diverse in its cultural settings and structure, of mission, worship and discipling.' For Land, one challenge of Pentecostal theology in our time is how the doctrine of holiness is to be communicated and received as a viable reference for personal and social righteousness.

Politics and justice are integral to our personal and social identities and, as such, are interrelated with our belief about personal and social holiness. Like all Christians, Pentecostals have a significant role to play in the world as 'salt and light'. He argues that the holiness, justice and goodness of God should be the benchmark for the choices we make in our private and public worlds. Failure to achieve this leads to apathy and disengagement with the true mission of believers, individually and collectively. Faith alone will not suffice.

The plea for rigorous training of the leadership is made in his consideration of Paul's epistles to Timothy. Pastors, in particular, are exhorted to take training seriously, and to seek all the training available in order to equip those they serve to engage in the confidence and the power of the Holy Spirit proclaimed by Pentecostals with the socio-political issues they encounter.

Land is emphatic in his view that our commitment to repentance and faith is a simultaneous commitment to discipleship and witness. He takes the unequivocal stance that discipleship not only should 'be taught with specific applications worked out in each culture and with each new generation but . . . [it] must [also] be lived out in the community . . .' Commitment to the Pentecostal heritage requires much more than 'church attendance' orchestrated by 'lone rangers'. As Land challenges, '[Pentecostal] Christians cannot be the light of the world while walking in darkness, ignoring injustice and dire human need, and practising the works of the flesh.' He cites 'compassionate care among and with the poor' as a reasonable starting point.

He is in agreement with the common observation that service rendered to the church is, more often than not, held higher than service to the wider community. Failure to engage with the issues of the day will distance us from those who care enough to seek to redress the wrongs in our world with the limited wisdom of humanity rather than divine wisdom. We may even be seen as naïve by the politically aware, regarded as victims rather than advocates of justice and righteousness.

According to conventional wisdom, questions inspire conversation and conversations enable learning and growth. Learning to ask the 'right' questions, engage in insightful conversations and then identify opportunities to practise what we believe, as Pentecostals, is clearly a positive way forward, if Land's argument is heeded. How we facilitate opportunities for meaningful conversations about social injustice between ourselves and other Christian and non-Christian faith groups, and put our declarations of faith into action are critical matters and challenges for our time.

Land makes the point that the 'Church of Pentecost was a new political power in the world' and asserts that Pentecostals 'must re-vision more deeply and reverently and transmit the faith that will sustain us in the more challenging days ahead'. Denominations such as the New Testament Church of God are taking this plea seriously and are seeking to establish opportunities to induct their 18–35-year-old members into active engagement and leadership roles within the various ministries of the Church, while others are strongly encouraging their young people to include theology in their advanced studies to better equip themselves for effectiveness in the effort to be 'salt and light' in the world. As Land emphasizes, theology matters in the choices we make: our engagement with the issues of the day will send messages to onlookers. Another contemporary challenge for us is how appealing the message of our brand of theology is to sceptics within and outside our movement. But perhaps a more important challenge is how far Pentecostal theology goes in words and deeds to augment a new and righteous beginning for the nations of our world.

# A Pentecostal appraisal of Scripture, reason, tradition and experience

The final chapter introduces and invites us to reflect on Pentecostal theology through the lens of the Wesleyan Quadrilateral. Developed to make the ramifications of theology more accessible to 'ordinary people', it offers, as Charlotte Johnson indicates, a useful tool for the interrogation of received wisdom.

Pentecostals hold Scripture to be the final authority for the Christian life. Scripture is the Word of God. The ministry of the Word is of vital importance for the personal and corporate life of the Pentecostal believer. In line with our Wesleyan roots, Pentecostals are in agreement that reason and reasoning are God-given gifts to make sense of the Word. Adherents are taught to read Scripture daily to discover God's directive for the day. The danger of unscrupulous interpretations of Scripture is obvious, particularly in our postmodern world when truth and lies are regarded as relative. As Johnson stipulates, there is an urgent need for those in the pews and pulpits to have practical access to Pentecostal theologians and scholars in order to help them understand and achieve their experience of the faith. Engagement in ecumenical efforts is cited as a favourable means to this end.

When considered from a holistic perspective, there can be no denial that Pentecostalism incorporates some of the traditions of the wider Christian Church, and rightly so. Ted Campbell's challenging instruction is used to support this point:

> Our calling, then, in recognizing the authority of tradition in a Wesleyan sense is not to favour an antiquated vision of the past; it is, rather, the calling to value God's own work throughout the story of God's people, and to take courage and confidence in the faithfulness of God speaking to us in tradition beyond the witness of the biblical age.[4]

Experience as referred to in the Wesleyan framework presents a means by which Pentecostals may process and articulate their Pentecostal experience objectively. As indicated in the first chapter, Pentecostal theology with its emphasis on believers' direct personal experience of God sets 'personal experience' and 'experiential knowledge' quite high among its precepts and formative processes. The subjectivity of experience and its manifestations can and do present challenges for the individuals concerned as well as the faith community, the Pentecostal movement itself and the witness of the wider Christian Church to the world. Reasoned Pentecostal theology will always provide a healthy resolution to clashes between intellectualism and spirituality. The Quadrilateral, in Johnson's observation, offers Pentecostals a 'structured approach' and a 'theological resource' for examining our theological stance, the way we do church now and what is to be taken forward by the next generation.

The five chapters in this book highlight a wide range of theological challenges that Pentecostals currently encounter within the movement and beyond. An underlying matter of concern throughout the discussions is that of succession planning in the missional focus of Pentecostals.

As with all challenges, there are opportunities. The Oliver Lyseight annual lecture is one opportunity in the effort to preserve our heritage and nurture the legacy of Pentecostalism. We address the challenges with a sense of urgency and concern in the hope of our faith. It is our aspiration that each chapter will stimulate further thinking and the willingness to engage more effectively in the prophetic ministry so strongly emphasized by our movement:

> And it shall come to pass in the last days, saith God, I will pour out of my Spirit upon all flesh: and your sons and your daughters shall prophesy, and your young men shall see visions, and your old men shall dream dreams: And on my servants and on my handmaidens I will pour out in those days of my Spirit; and they shall prophesy.
> (Acts 2.17–18)

John Maxwell and others have given much consideration to how thinking, attitudes and behaviour interrelate. They promote the view that when we challenge our thinking and beliefs, we open ourselves to new ways of thinking, new possibilities, new beginnings.[5] Pentecostals, like all other members of the Christian family, are sometimes accused of not always preaching what we practise or practising what we preach. This book encourages us as Christians, and in particular as Pentecostals, to be courageous in our pilgrimage and seize opportunities to reconsider and reinterpret our conventional wisdom and theology to reinvigorate our credibility, growth and sustainability. The process may cause discomfort, anxiety, even crises of faith – all hallmarks of growth, from childhood, through adolescence to adulthood. In the interest of growth and maturity, may we be enabled to embrace the challenges we face as opportunities for development in the faith and our missional focus.

## Notes

1 José Daniel Montañez, 'My Pentecostal Experience: Fire that carries us through the fire', *Church of God Evangel* (September 2019), p. 21.
2 M. M. Poloma, 'Glossolalia, Liminality and Empowered Kingdom Building: A sociological perspective', in M. Cartledge (ed.), *Speaking in Tongues: Multi-disciplinary perspectives* (Carlisle: Paternoster Press, 2006), p. 151.
3 W. K. Kay, *Pentecostalism: A very short introduction* (Oxford: Oxford University Press, 2011), p. 57.
4 T. A. Campbell, 'Authority and the Wesleyan Quadrilateral' in C. Yrigoyen Jr (ed.), *The T&T Clark Companion to Methodism* (London: T&T Clark, 2014).
5 See John C. Maxwell, *Thinking for a Change: 11 ways highly successful people approach life and work* (New York: Warner Books, 2003).

# 1

# The quest for a Pentecostal theology: a theology of encounter

## KEITH WARRINGTON

## What is a Pentecostal?

Just over a hundred years ago, Pentecostalism was born. Since then, it has developed to become one of the biggest and fastest growing components of Christianity.[1] It's big – but it's not what it was. There are so many different streams – classical Pentecostal, neo-Pentecostal and independent Pentecostal churches – that it now takes two dictionaries, one of which has been revised, and a regular supply of books and articles to try to do justice to exploring them.[2] Also, although originally a largely Western movement, it is now increasingly represented by people from the majority world.[3] Sixty-six per cent of Pentecostals now live in the majority world; 87 per cent live in poorer areas of the world; 71 per cent are non-white.[4] Increasingly, it is more accurate to identify Pentecostalism in the plural form – Pentecostalisms – as there is no longer a set framework into which all Pentecostals easily fit.

The very diversity of Pentecostalism means that it is less identifiable than it once was. Some of its most distinctive beliefs (including baptism in the Spirit, and speaking in tongues and its place as the initial evidence of the baptism in the Spirit) are less distinctive in Pentecostalism than they were; at the same time, some of the foundational elements of Pentecostalism are now also present in the lives of many non-Pentecostal believers. The rise of renewal movements and neo-Pentecostalism has blurred the dividing lines. Yong concludes, 'It is difficult, if not well-nigh impossible, to "essentialize" Pentecostalism conceptually.'[5] Furthermore, what it means to be Pentecostal varies depending on the continent, tradition or denomination and the experience of the Spirit for the individual concerned.[6] Even umbrella organizations, such as the Pentecostal World Conference, do not incorporate all (or even most) of the many Pentecostal groups in the world.[7] Hollenweger writes, 'I do not know anybody who could convincingly define what mainstream Pentecostalism is', an issue compounded by the fact that despite their differences, 'most Pentecostal denominations believe themselves to be mainstream.'[8]

# What is the Pentecostal DNA?

## Theology

Some have sought to identify Pentecostals on the basis of their beliefs[9] comprising Jesus as Saviour, healer, baptizer and coming king,[10] to which is sometimes added the sanctifying role of Jesus[11] or the concept of blessing, the latter being a distinctive contribution of Yonggi Cho.[12] More to the point, most Pentecostal beliefs are also accepted by millions of Charismatic believers.

## Encounter

However, that which is fundamental to Pentecostalism is a personal, experiential encounter with the Spirit of God.[13] Pentecostals aim to know God experientially, whether it is via an intellectual recognition of his being or an emotional appreciation of his character. It is this that often makes Pentecostalism functionally different as a Christian tradition. Pentecostals have always emphasized experiential Christianity rather than doctrinal confession. That is why, in the earliest days, Pentecostals were comfortable with ecumenical relationships, because the common experience of the Spirit was more important than different beliefs; traditionally, they refused to adopt creeds and statements of faith because there was a fear that they might crush the quest for experience. Pentecostals look for expressions of life and vitality in their faith. The sense of the immediate, of the God of the now not the distant past, is a characteristic that underlies how they do theology. Pentecostal theology is a theology of the dynamic, seen through the lens of experience. It is a functional theology that exists to operate in an experiential dimension. Pentecostals embrace a spirituality that expects to touch God and to be touched by him. For Pentecostals, to know God is to experience him, not just intellectualize him.

Central to their spirituality is Pentecostals' expectation of experiencing the Spirit in their lives. It is this that best identifies the Pentecostal heartbeat. Christenson describes Pentecostalism as 'Christianity standing on tiptoe, expecting something to happen'.[14] Hollenweger deduces that Pentecostalism is best expressed as providing an opportunity for believers to engage in 'an adventure in fellowship with the Holy Spirit and each other'.[15] The Spirit offers the possibility of a journey of discovery, a quest for a destiny, an exploration of the inexplicable that will touch and transform our lives . . . remarkable.

# Pentecostals are losing their expectation of such encounters with the Spirit

The Spirit is in danger of being marginalized and his ability to change the lives of believers is being overlooked.

Some reasons why we miss the Spirit in our lives as believers, in my view, are the following:

- He has sometimes been valued more for his gifts than for who he is.
- He is so associated with the baptism in the Spirit and spiritual gifts, especially speaking in tongues, that many assume he has little else to offer.
- His description as the 'Holy *Ghost*' has been another hindrance to his being better appreciated as a personal mentor to believers. He has no name and no body and so we struggle to identify with him. However, although he cannot smile, we can know his joy; he may not be able to cry, but he feels sadness; he may have no ears, but he hears our softest cry; he may have no eyes, but he sees us even in a crowd and also sees how we feel when nobody else does; he may have no personal name, but he is not anonymous. He may be understood as a force but he is also our friend.
- Some are unsure as to whether he should be worshipped. Too often, he is viewed as simply 'the third person of the trinity', generally mentioned after the Father and Jesus, unhelpfully suggesting a divine hierarchy. In the Old Testament, he is largely (but not completely) absent. However, the Spirit is not subservient to the Father or Jesus. He is not their divine servant nor is he less deserving of our worship, service and honour. He is God (Matthew 28.19; Luke 1.35; 1 Corinthians 3.16; 1 Thessalonians 4.8).
- Many Pentecostals are uncertain as to how they should address him and wonder if it is appropriate to pray to him.
- Many misunderstand his relationship to believers, assuming that he is involved in their lives mainly to use them to achieve divinely inspired objectives and to catch them when they sin. Although he does empower believers and is involved in the disciplinary process for the benefit of Christians, these are not his only or main emphases.

- Many Pentecostals assume that he rarely speaks and that if he did, he would speak to others and through others, neither to them nor through them. Very often, believers assume that Jesus walks with them and the Father guides them but the Spirit has little practical relevance – other than on those rare occasions when he has a temporary impact on them. However, the Spirit is more important, more central, more immanently involved with believers, more often and more regularly, more intentionally and strategically than most realize. They just don't know what they are missing.

# How do Pentecostals experience the Spirit?

In what ways do Pentecostals expect to experience and encounter the Spirit? This has traditionally been best exemplified in the baptism in the Spirit, sometimes manifested by speaking in tongues. However, there has been a decrease in the numbers of people who claim to have experienced the baptism in the Spirit, especially in the West, to which may be added the fact that the experience is only encouraged to a limited extent by Pentecostal leaders. The Pew Forum on Religion and Public Life, a hugely significant research organization, undertook a ten-country survey concerning Pentecostal practice and belief. This related to the USA, Brazil, Chile, Guatemala, Kenya, Nigeria, South Africa, India, the Philippines and South Korea. Its findings make for very interesting reading. In particular, in six of these countries, more than four in ten said they never speak in tongues. The figure for Pentecostals who never speak in tongues in the USA is 49 per cent. Poloma writes, 'In some Classical Pentecostal circles, glossolalia is in danger of becoming a doctrine devoid of experience with an estimated 50% or more of followers reporting that they do not speak in tongues.'[16] If the baptism in the Spirit and speaking in tongues are the clearest evidences of the working of the Spirit for contemporary Pentecostals, we have a problem – because both of them are less prominent in many Pentecostal communities than they were. If these encounters are believed to be the most likely ways whereby Pentecostals experience the Spirit and they are decreasing in frequency, we face a major challenge.

# Do Pentecostals know what the Spirit has to offer?

The Spirit is a comprehensive resource for the believer but too many are not aware of this. The bestowal of the Spirit on believers was much more comprehensive after Pentecost than before, but do Pentecostals know this?

- The Spirit is committed to proactively transforming believers. He is integrally related to the process of salvation, committed to setting believers apart, affirming them, transforming them ethically and spiritually, inspiring and empowering them. He energizes them, creating faith, motivating sanctification and inspiring prayer. Do Pentecostals know this experientially?
- The Spirit provides comprehensive, limitless resources for believers with regard to their salvation. He is the one who makes it possible for people to enter the kingdom of God (John 3.5–6), to know that they are adopted (Romans 8.15–16), with all the privileges and responsibilities of that fact, and to relate to God as Father, experiencing eternal life from the start of that relationship. His presence in their lives is the evidence that believers are authentic children of God (Romans 8.9). Do Pentecostals know what these are?
- The Spirit provides resources and gifts for all believers and expects them to be used and to be used sensitively for every task he sets, diversely distributing gifts to function for the benefit of all in the development of the Church, inspiring and

initiating evangelism, preaching, prophecy and other cha-
rismata.[17] He brings liberty, inspires joy, wisdom, faith, truth
and revelation, among other gifts. How many Pentecostals are
accessing these gifts and how many are guided in the process?

# So here is our challenge

Our Pentecostal DNA suggests that we desire encounters with
the Spirit. Our Pentecostal praxis indicates that such encounters
are narrowly focused; in truth, most Pentecostals do not anticipate they will encounter the Spirit often or much. They are only
aware of a very small capacity of the Spirit's agenda for them.
Too often they think of the Spirit as Cinderella who comes to the
ball late, leaves early and deposits something small – precious,
but small – in their lives. Thereafter, like Cinderella, he must be
searched for – in the hope that he may give more in the future –
but too often that is only for the princely few. To anticipate that
he could be interested in actually being their personal mentor
and guiding light is a limited expectation for most Pentecostals.
The Spirit is assumed to be too busy to spend his valuable time
with us. And the devil smirks as we turn up the volume and
listen for guidance elsewhere when the Spirit has never stopped
directing us to the destiny that he has set for us.

# How can Pentecostals encounter the Spirit more?
## He is more than a force – he's our friend

He's a person – not a liquid. We don't drink him in or breathe
him in – or smell him. To many, he has become a powerful
source of energy rather than a personal guide, a miraculous
force rather than a mentoring friend. He has been largely viewed
functionally as the one who can facilitate the believer to be a

useful disciple of Jesus. But he's more than that – much more. He's our friend.

## He's more than the baptism in the Spirit

Although Pentecostals stress that the baptism in the Spirit does not indicate that believers are devoid of the Spirit until they experience it, this message has not always been carefully disseminated. Traditionally, Pentecostals have separated the Spirit from the act of salvation to such an extent that it has been difficult to deduce his role in salvation; indeed, the implicit understanding for many has been that his influence in the life of the believer is limited or even non-existent until the occurrence of the baptism in the Spirit. This has led many of those who have not received the baptism in the Spirit to be disappointed and even marginalized as somehow lacking in the best that God has to offer, their Christianity second class, despite the quality of their spirituality or even the effectiveness of their witness. An inappropriate presentation of the baptism in the Spirit can result in it appearing to be dangerously elitist.[18] While not denigrating the baptism in the Spirit, or any other Spirit-inspired experience, it is crucial to enable believers to experientially and intellectually realize the Spirit-inspired event of conversion and his involvement in their lives thereafter. Furthermore, to suggest that all believers are indwelt by the Spirit but that only those who have received the baptism in the Spirit are empowered by him undermines the richness of the resources of the Spirit made available to all believers at salvation. The Spirit entered our lives at conversion and began his work of transforming us then. His involvement in our lives should result in our experiencing the Spirit on multiple occasions throughout our lives, bringing about a multi-layered bestowal of the Spirit depending on our given needs or his sovereign manifestation. There is a continuing need for us to recognize that whether or not we have been baptized in the Spirit, we are to develop our walk with the Spirit, as an integral element of our spiritual journeys.

## He is more than power

In concentrating on power, Pentecostals are in danger of viewing their Christian experience as best defined by concepts of strength, victory and charismatically enabled progress (*theologia gloriae*) while forgetting that the latter also occur in times of weakness (Romans 8.7–8, 23, 35–7; 2 Corinthians 4.7–11; 6.4–10; 12.7–10), eclipse and even apparent defeat (*theologia crucis*).

## He wants to encounter us . . .

Fundamentally, we need to revisit what the Bible says about the Spirit and prepare ourselves to be surprised about what we will discover. Many Pentecostals are in danger of existing in a spiritual desert – devoid of the Spirit, except on the rare occasions when the Spirit breaks through into their lives or they break into his. For many, there exists an assumption that this is normal. For too long, they have believed the myth that the Spirit only rarely encounters believers. The truth is he's doing it all the time; we just assume that would be too good to be true – but it isn't. We have believed the lie that the Spirit only guides special people. We would be shocked to be told that he thinks that believers are special. Too often we miss him because, first, we never knew he is so determined to be on our side; second, we did not realize that his prime aim is to do us good; and third, because of both those assumptions, we don't listen for him to speak to us. Of fundamental importance is the fact that the Spirit is on our side and thus, to be encountered and experienced.

### . . . through the Bible

The way that Pentecostals read the Bible has been, and still is, to a degree, unique in that they anticipate that its main values are to help them develop their experience of God. This is more important to Pentecostals than its value as a resource for the identification and elaboration of various doctrines. Although they would state that they hold to an orthodox theology, few would see the establishment of that as the main purpose of the Bible. Instead, the Bible is viewed primarily as a place of encounter; an encounter with the divine author. It is recognized as a collection of stories intended to lead a person to God and to be transformed as a result – rather than to be a database of dogma to be discussed. Pentecostals expect to encounter God personally as they read it.[19] The Bible is less to be studied and more to be seen as the altar of sacrifice to which they bring their lives for renewal. Conscious attempts are made to locate 'a word from the Lord' in all parts of the text. This is not motivated by a perverse intent to identify obtuse interpretations; rather, it is based on a belief that God desires to reveal his word which is by nature dynamic and life-giving. The Bible is anticipated as being for the purpose of touching its readers emotionally, not so much to teach them intellectually; to result in an experience, not merely better exegesis; to result in an exposure of God not only an exposition of truth.

How do we listen to the Spirit in the text?

- Ask questions of the text – why are you saying this, Matthew? Why did you say this, John, when Matthew, Mark and Luke left it out? Why, Paul, do you refer to being baptized in the Spirit in different ways from Luke? As well as asking questions of the text, I am also asking questions of the Spirit of the text.
- Be aware that the Spirit may speak additionally to the message that he supervised thousands of years ago. Be prepared to be wowed by what you discover. This is a dynamic text; it's to be engaged with, explored, discovered, not treated like a text-book, a dogmatic treatise of facts. It's Spirit-filled: not static or stagnant – but dynamic.
- Treat sermons as opportunities to share what you have discovered as a result of the adventure you have taken with the Spirit. Remember that preaching/teaching is a trialogue – you, the audience and the Spirit. In preaching,

include others in the process; risk thinking through the text with a colleague; include the congregation in the process. Let's demonstrate that. Don't lock the Spirit out of it or assume that praying he'll speak through you is enough, or that what he said in the study is all he will have to say. He may want to inspire you as you speak. Partner him in the process. That means you may have to speak and listen at the same time; you may have to speak and watch your audience in order to see what the Spirit is doing in them; you may have to pause to attune your thoughts to the Spirit's agenda. Explore with others how the Spirit encounters you in the text and vice versa.

### . . . outside the Bible

Although the Bible is a fundamentally important source of guidance, it does not exist to provide answers to every question that may be posed. It was fundamentally written for readers who existed in ancient cultures and eras that are inevitably different from those of later generations. Therefore, to view it as the basis for all decision-making for all times, even with reference to the life and practices of believers, is not always appropriate. When the Bible is not and cannot be an influential guide, the Spirit is. Paul encourages his readers to 'live by the Spirit' (Galatians 5.25), 'walk by the Spirit' (Galatians 5.16, 25), and 'be filled with the Spirit' (Ephesians 5.18), as a result of which they will develop godly lifestyles. The Spirit may choose to speak through the language of the Bible but he may as easily speak in other ways (John 15.7–12; Acts 15.28).[20] Land argues that the Spirit 'speaks scripturally but also has more to say than Scripture'.[21] That is not to suggest that the Spirit is superior to the Word or the Word to the Spirit. The Spirit and the Word function together, on occasion the former through the latter but also sometimes spontaneously and without specific reference to the written Word.[22] The Spirit thus provides a canon outside the canon in a relentless river of revelation that includes the vitally important biblical text.

However, where the Spirit functions outside the written Word, caveats must be carefully instituted in order to check for errors in the listening process.[23] Thus, extra-biblical revelation must be assessed in the context of the Christian community which has itself been developed by the Spirit and the Word (1 Corinthians 12.3; 14.29; 1 John 4.1–3).[24] An example of the Spirit-community model in identifying the will of God is reflected in Acts 15.22, 28. Thomas and Shelton explore the Jerusalem council and note the role of the community in arriving at the conclusion to welcome Gentiles into the Church.[25] Where there was uncertainty and limited scriptural guidance, the believers looked to the Spirit to facilitate the correct conclusion.

People don't hear the Spirit because they are not expecting him to speak, or they only expect him to speak to certain people or on special occasions or when we're in need or on a spiritual high. What happens is that the Spirit speaks but we are not trained to listen. So . . .

- expect the Spirit to speak – to you – every day;
- make time to listen and review what the Spirit reveals about God and his intentions for us;
- when praying for people (the sick, for example), take time to listen for the Spirit's guidance – and let the people know that you are listening.

### . . . in the Christian community

Guidance is best determined in the context of a community of believers and the wider Church, past and present and different from our own.[26] It provides the opportunity for balance and accountability while protecting us from subjective tendencies.[27] So, in our local churches:

- discuss ways (among leaders and attendees) whereby the Spirit can be facilitated;
- intentionally provide room for the Spirit,
- make sermons opportunities for Spirit-led encounters;
- encourage people to anticipate the Spirit in evangelism;
- help people to be creative as is the Spirit;
- reintroduce testimonies to reflect various aspects of the work of the Spirit;
- refresh the way we structure our services and introduce opportunities for the Spirit;
- ask people to listen for him in their daily lives . . . and share what he has taught them;
- interview people by asking some of the questions identified earlier (have a microphone at the front of the church and a roving one);
- revisit occasions where traditionally we expect him (prayer for the weak, baptism in the Spirit encounters, the Lord's Supper, speaking in tongues, gifts of the Spirit);
- learn from our (Pentecostal) traditions – the past;
- our traditions have value; don't dismantle them too quickly. When I was much younger, although I didn't realize it, I lived according to a Pentecostal creed that sometimes offered advice on issues about which the Bible was silent – they were very important to me. Those guidelines informed my behaviour in terms of what I should do and should not do. Much of these guidelines is still valuable today but they are being eroded;
- learn from the Pentecostal academic community. Scholars can help us when we read the text, reminding us of its original context before we contextualize it for ourselves. If we do both exercises, it will help us make sense of it;
- learn from other Christian communities, different from our own;
- learn from different cultures. Pentecostals need to take advantage of what the Spirit is also saying to others in different cultures from our own.

### . . . in partnership with him

- Teach believers that gifts are given for the benefit of others and that they are intended to enable us to partner the Spirit;
- help believers identify their Spirit-given gifts and ministries;
- remind believers of their diversity;
- remind believers that God has already gifted them;
- facilitate opportunities for believers' gifts to be used.

# Conclusion

Too many Pentecostals do not hear the Spirit because they are not expecting him to speak, or they only expect him to speak to certain people or on special occasions, or when they may be in a particular difficult situation or on a spiritual high. In reality, the Spirit is speaking more than most realize, but they have not been trained to listen. A little while ago, I had the privilege of sharing dinner with Dr David Yonggi Cho and his wife, the president of Hansei University, where I had been invited to speak. David is the founder of the largest church in the world, located in Yoido, South Korea, and part of the Full Gospel denomination. His church alone has 700 missionaries and 400 pastors, plus other leaders; the sanctuary seats 12,000 people and they have multiple services each Sunday which are broadcast throughout Seoul and beyond. In our conversation, I asked him what was central to his theology and life. Two fundamental motifs, he said, undergird his life and mission. One is that God is good; the other is to partner with the Spirit. He describes the Spirit as his senior partner and regularly advocates spending time with the Spirit. He affirms, 'I acknowledge the Holy Spirit in every matter. As a result, I experience the work of the Holy Spirit.' Indeed, he identifies the reason for his pastoral success as 'personal fellowship with the Holy Spirit'. He acknowledges that a vision he received in 1964 stimulated this development; in it, God revealed to him that he needed to have fellowship with the Spirit, as a result of which his perception of the Spirit changed 'from "power" to "person"'.

All believers are privileged to partner the Spirit and listen to him as he reminds us of our status and our potential. The same Spirit who created the universe is actively and intimately involved in our lives. He does not idly sit by and watch the world from a distance; he prefers to move dynamically within us, developing fresh experiences, providing unique lessons, innovative opportunities, progressive adventures, imaginative prospects, creating what we will be out of what we are – creating opportunities for us to encounter him. Pentecostals have a DNA, a heartbeat, a central core to their being – it is the desire to encounter the Spirit. Our challenge is not to assume that the Spirit rarely desires to provide these encounters with him.

The privilege granted to all believers is to listen to the Spirit through the Word, dynamically and immediately; to listen to him through other believers in and out of our communities; to listen for him in life and do so often; and to take time to teach others how to do the same. He is an endless source of exploration and we will never finally close the book on describing him completely. However, as children who are presented with a delightful treasure, he draws us to himself to enjoy him for ever. We may run towards him or tentatively tiptoe in his direction, looking over our shoulders as if we are still uncertain whether this is ground that is too holy for us. However we approach him, the one thing we can be certain of is a welcome – a coming home to the one who already has us in his heart.

## Notes

1 The journal *Heritage* is dedicated to the history of the AOG (<www.AGHeritage.org>) in association with the Flower Pentecostal Heritage Centre. See also M. W. Dempster, B. D. Klaus, D. Petersen

(eds), *The Globalization of Pentecostalism: A religion made to travel* (Oxford: Regnum Books, 1999), pp. 85–115; H. B. Smith (ed.), *Pentecostals from the Inside Out* (Wheaton, IL: Victory, 1990); C. H. Mason, *History and Formative Years of the Church of God in Christ with Excerpts from the Life and Works of its Founder: Bishop C. H. Mason* (Memphis, TN: Church of God in Christ Publishing House, 1973); A. Clayton, 'The Significance of William H. Durham for Pentecostal Historiography', *Pneuma* 1.2 (1970), pp. 27–42; J. R. Goff, *Fields White unto Harvest: Charles F. Parham and the missionary origins of Pentecostalism* (Fayetteville, AR: University of Arkansas Press, 1988); N. Bloch-Hoell, *The Pentecostal Movement: Its origin, development, and distinctive character* (Oslo: Allen and Unwin, 1964); E. A. Wilson, *Strategy of the Spirit: J. Philip Hogan and the growth of the Assemblies of God worldwide 1960-1990* (Carlisle: Regnum, 1997); E. L. Blumhofer, *The Assemblies of God: A chapter in the story of American Pentecostalism*, 2 vols. (Springfield, MO: Gospel Publishing House, 1989).

2 See <www.keithwarrington.co.uk>; also the various articles in S. M. Burgess, E. M. Van der Maas (eds), *The New International Dictionary of Pentecostal and Charismatic Movements* (Grand Rapid, MIs: Zondervan, 2002); S. Burgess (ed.), *Encyclopedia of Pentecostal and Charismatic Christianity* (London: Routledge, 2006); C. E. Jones, *A Guide to the Study of the Pentecostalism*, 2 vols (Metuchen, NJ: Scarecrow Press, 1983).

3 K. Larbi, 'African Pentecostalism in the Context of Global Pentecostal Ecumenical Fraternity: Challenges and opportunities', *Pneuma* 24.2 (2002), pp. 138–66; W. Hollenweger, *The Pentecostals: The Charismatic movement in the churches* (Minneapolis, MN: Augsburg, 1972), pp. 1–74; J. Tinney, 'Black Origins of the Pentecostal Movement', *Christianity Today* 16.1 (1971), pp. 4–6; C. E. Jones, *Black Holiness: A guide to the study of Black participation in Wesleyan perfectionistic and glossolalic Pentecostal movements* (Metuchen, NJ: Scarecrow Press, 1987).

4 J. H. Logan Jr, 'Black Pentecostalism', in Burgess (ed.), *Encyclopedia of Pentecostal and Charismatic Christianity*, pp. 60–4.

5 A. Yong, '"Not Knowing Where The Wind Blows . . .": On envisioning a Pentecostal-Charismatic theology of religions', *Journal of Pentecostal Theology* 14 (April 1999), p. 94.

6 W. Ma, 'Toward an Asian Pentecostal Theology', *Cyberjournal for Pentecostal-Charismatic Research* 1 (1998).

7 C. T. Thomas, 'Pentecostal Theology in the Twenty-First Century: 1998 Presidential Address to the Society for Pentecostal Studies', *Pneuma* 21 (1998), pp. 3–19.

8 W. Hollenweger, 'Pentecostalism: Past, Present and Future', *Journal of the European Pentecostal Theological Association* 21 (2001), p. 46.

9 J. T. Nichol, *Pentecostalism* (Plainfield, NJ: Logos, 1966), pp. 2–3; R. H. Hughes, *What Is Pentecost?* (Cleveland, TN: Pathway Press, 1963); R. H. Hughes, *Church of God Distinctives* (Cleveland: Pathway Press, 1968, 1989); M. S. Clark, H. I. Lederle (eds), *What Is Distinctive about Pentecostal Theology?* (Pretoria: University of South Africa, 1989), pp. 143–52; R. Cotton, 'What Does It Mean to Be Pentecostal? Three perspectives: the dynamic behind the doctrine', *Paraclete* 28.3 (1994), p. 12.

10 W. Vondey, 'Christian Amnesia: Who in the world are Pentecostals?', *Asian Journal of Pentecostal Studies* 4.1 (2001), pp. 32–4; G. Wacker, 'Wild Theories and Mad Excitement', in Smith (ed.), *Pentecostals from the Inside Out*, p. 21; F. Macchia, 'Theology, Pentecostal', in Burgess and Van der Maas (eds), *New International Dictionary of Pentecostal and Charismatic Movements*, p. 1124.

11 S. Land, *Pentecostal Spirituality: A passion for the kingdom* (Sheffield: Sheffield Academic Press, 1993), p. 18; J. C. Thomas, 'Pentecostal Theology in the Twenty-First Century: 1998 Presidential Address to the Society for Pentecostal Studies', *Pneuma* 21 (1998), pp. 3–19. For a critique, see T. Cross, 'Can There Be a Pentecostal Systematic Theology? An essay on theological method in a post-modern world' in *Teaching to Make Disciples: Education for Pentecostal-Charismatic Spirituality and Life: The collected papers of the 30th annual meeting of the SPS* (Tulsa, OK: Oral Roberts University, 2001), pp. 145–66.

12 D. Yonggi Cho, *Five-fold Gospel and Three-fold Blessing* (Seoul: Young San Publishing, 1983).

13 V.-M. Kärkkäinen, '"The Re-Turn of Religion in the Third Millennium": Pentecostalisms and postmodernities', European Pentecostal Charismatic Research Association Conference paper, University of Uppsala, 2007, p. 5; H. Zegwaart, 'Christian Experience in Community', *Cyberjournal for Pentecostal-Charismatic Research* 11 (2002); D. E. Albrecht, *Rites in the Spirit: A ritual approach to*

*Pentecostal/Charismatic spirituality* (Sheffield: Sheffield Academic Press, 1999), p. 10; G. L. Anderson, 'Pentecostals Believe in More than Tongues', in Smith (ed.), *Pentecostals from the Inside Out*, pp. 55–6; J. K. Asamoah-Gyadu, 'An African Pentecostal on Mission in Eastern Europe: The Church of the "Embassy of God" in the Ukraine', *Pneuma* 27.2 (2005), p. 314; T. L. Cross, 'A Proposal to Break the Ice: What can Pentecostal theology offer Evangelical theology?', *Journal of Pentecostal Theology* 10.2 (2002), pp. 49–58. For a non-Pentecostal Roman Catholic enquiry into the relationship between power, experience and the Spirit, see B. Cooke, *Power and the Spirit of God: Toward an experience-based pneumatology* (Oxford: Oxford University Press, 2004).

14 L. Christenson, 'Pentecostalism's Forgotten Forerunner', in V. Synan (ed.), *Aspects of Pentecostal-Charismatic Origins* (Plainfield, NJ: Logos International, 1975), p. 27.

15 Hollenweger, 'Pentecostalism: Past, Present and Future', pp. 43–5.

16 M. M. Poloma, 'Glossolalia, Liminality and Empowered Kingdom Building: A sociological perspective', in M. J. Cartledge (ed.), *Speaking in Tongues: Multi-disciplinary perspectives* (Carlisle: Paternoster Press, 2006), p. 151.

17 Examples of charismatic endowments by the Spirit are also located in the Old Testament: strength (Judg. 14.6, 19; 15.14); leadership (Gen. 41.38; Isa. 11.1–3); military authority (Judg. 6.34; 11.29–33); skill (Exod. 31.3–4; 35.31); wisdom (Dan. 5.14); prophecy (Num. 11.25, 29; 24.2; 1 Sam. 10.10; 19.19–24; Mic. 3.8). See also W. Ma, 'The Empowerment of the Spirit of God in Luke-Acts: An Old Testament perspective', in W. Ma and W. Menzies (eds), *The Spirit and Spirituality: Essays in honour of Russell P. Spittler* (Sheffield: Sheffield Academic Press, 2004), pp. 28–34; G. J. Leeper, 'The Nature of the Pentecostal Gift with Special Reference to Numbers 11 and Acts 2', *AJPS* 6.1 (2003), pp. 23–38.

18 Thus, W. D. Collins, in 'An Assemblies of God Perspective on Demonology. Part 2', *Paraclete* 28.1 (1994), p. 22, writes, 'When a believer is baptized in the Holy Spirit, he is anointed . . . so he can move against the works of the devil as Christ did', as if this only relates to those who have been baptized in the Spirit.

19 V. Synan, 'Pentecostalism: Varieties and contributions', *Pneuma* 9.1 (1987), p. 39.

20 J. W. Wyckoff, 'The Inspiration and Authority of Scripture', in J. K. Bridges (ed.), *The Bible, the Word of God* (Springfield, MO: Gospel Publishing House, 2003), p. 24.

21 Land, *Pentecostal Spirituality*, p. 100; K. J. Archer, *A Pentecostal Hermeneutic for the Twenty-First Century: Spirit, Scripture and community* (London: Continuum, 2004), p. 147.

22 Land, *Pentecostal Spirituality*, pp. 100, 118; Archer, *A Pentecostal Hermeneutic*, p. 80; J. Ruthven, 'A Place for Prophecy', *Paraclete* 6.2 (1972), pp. 8–14; W. A. Grudem, 'Can All Believers Prophesy?', *Paraclete* 15.4 (1981), pp. 11–14.

23 See V.-M. Kärkkäinen and A. Yong, *Toward a Pneumatologial Theology: Pentecostal and ecumenical perspectives on ecclesiology, soteriology and theology of mission* (Lanham, MD: University Press of America, 2002), p. 14; T. Cargal, 'Beyond the Fundamentalist–Modernist Controversy: Pentecostals and hermeneutics in a postmodern age', *Pneuma* 15.2 (1993), pp. 173–4.

24 M. D. McLean, 'Toward a Pentecostal Hermeneutic', *Pneuma* 6 (1984), p. 50.

25 J. C. Thomas, 'Women, Pentecostals and the Bible: An experiment in Pentecostal hermeneutics', *Journal of Pentecostal Theology* 5 (1994), pp. 44–50; J. B. Shelton, 'Epistemology and Authority in the Acts of the Apostles: An analysis and test case study of Acts 15:1–29', *Spirit and Church* 2.2 (2000), pp. 231–47.

26 Archer, *A Pentecostal Hermeneutic*; see also D. Coulter, 'What Meaneth This? Pentecostals and Theological Enquiry', *Journal of Pentecostal Theology* 10.1 (October 2001), pp. 62–3; L. G. McClung, 'Explosion, Motivation, and Consolidation: The historical anatomy of a missionary movement', in L. G. McClung Jr (ed.), *Azusa Street and Beyond* (South Plainfield, NJ: Bridge Publishing House, 1986), pp. 6–7; C. Pinnock, 'The Work of the Holy Spirit in Hermeneutics', *Journal of Pentecostal Theology* 2 (1993), pp. 16–17; S. A. Ellington, 'Pentecostalism and the Authority of Scripture', *Journal of Pentecostal Theology* 9 (1996), p. 29; R. D. Israel, D. E. Albrecht and R. G. McNally, 'Pentecostals and Hermeneutics: Texts, Rituals and Community', *Pneuma* 15.2 (1993), pp. 154–61; S. K. H. Chan, *Pentecostal Theology and the Christian Spiritual Tradition* (Sheffield: Sheffield Academic Press, 2000), p. 44.

27 Chan, *Pentecostal Theology*, p. 45.

# 2

# Pentecostal spirituality in our postmodern world

## DOUGLAS NELSON

God hath chosen the foolish things of the world to confound
the wise; and God hath chosen the weak things of the world
to confound the things which are mighty; And base things of
the world, and things which are despised, hath God chosen,
yea, and things which are not, to bring to nought things that
are: That no flesh should glory in His presence.
(1 Corinthians 1.27–29)

Modern Pentecostal spirituality burst forth in 1906 from a small
Bible study and prayer meeting of devout black Christians, in
a modest home in Los Angeles, California. They were led by a
serious black Christian minister (and later bishop), William J.
Seymour, seeking the power of the original Christian faith given
to the apostles by our Lord Christ Jesus, as described in Jude 3.
Soon, in answer to prayer, the power of almighty God fell upon
this little group, resulting in an amazingly rapid national and
global outreach. Large incoming crowds of interested persons
and curious onlookers from a cross-section of the city overwhelmed the small house.

They moved to a new location at 312 Azusa Street, site
of a former black church and latterly a storage warehouse.
To accommodate the large crowds, often up to 1,500 at a
time, daily meetings were begun, from early mornings to

late at night. Overflow crowds stood outside at the building's windows.

Within weeks, the first overseas missionaries departed for Scandinavia, India and China, and were soon followed by others to Africa and elsewhere. The group's newspaper, *The Apostolic Faith*, launched with an initial printing of 5,000 copies, reached a circulation of 50,000 by 1908. Copies were sometimes passed from hand to hand until they fell apart.

The term 'Pentecostal movement' stems from Seymour's own usage. He joyfully exclaimed, 'We are on the verge of the greatest miracle the world has ever seen.'[1] Today, what started as a small prayer group of black Christians has reached over 612 million adherents worldwide,[2] and is still growing strongly.

The secret strength of this amazing explosion of Pentecostal spirituality lay in the depths of the black soul: an appreciation for the sacred words of our inspired Holy Bible, coupled with a longing for the power of the original apostolic faith, and much genuine Christian love, born amid the terrible sufferings of slavery. Out of that suffering came a Christian faith embodying the very deepest meaning of Christian love, a love that suffers long, and is kind (1 Corinthians 13.4).

During this black Christian-originated outburst of Pentecostal spirituality, persons of all social standing and racial backgrounds came together harmoniously on Azusa Street with significant loving concern for one another. For the several years of the Azusa revival, the evils of racial separation were laid aside in the name and power of the Lord.

Led by the remarkable William J. Seymour, it was a shining moment of Christian love crossing the colour line. Seymour was an extraordinary leader of monumental Pentecostal spirituality, empowered by Christ-like love. His leadership demonstrated profound Bible understanding and gifted pastoral leadership. Seymour was the very embodiment of that truly Christian love that has suffered long, but which in return expresses great kindness. He exemplified the rare virtues of meekness and lowliness set forth by our Lord himself (Matthew 11.29).

It is unlikely that anyone else could have accomplished what Seymour did. He led the greatest Christian revival of the twentieth century and arguably the greatest of all time, in terms of its explosive power, reaching to every part of the world. It continues to grow to this very day. Above all else, Seymour was determined to 'contend for the faith once delivered unto the saints' (Jude 3). His Christian Pentecostal spirituality held forth at the centre of that revival until it took on a life of its own with the power to reach around the world even after he was forgotten, a prophet without honour in his own time.

When, because of the racial separations that followed the Azusa Street revival, the white Christians departed from their black brothers and sisters, the love of racial togetherness was lost. Seymour was forgotten. Although the revival dynamic remained as a tribute to his truly meek and humble Christ-like love, gained from his response to the terrible sufferings of black Americans, most historical accounts of this great revival overlook Seymour's leadership because of his colour.

The white Pentecostals who departed from the Azusa revival behaved very differently from those courageous Christians who were formed from the original Day of Pentecost 2,000 years ago. Back then, the Christians were known for their new brand of love, an amazing love that enabled them to stand ready to die for their Lord and for one another. Those magnificent Christians remained dedicated to the divine command of our Lord:

A new commandment I give unto you, That ye love one another; as I have loved you, that ye also love one another. By this shall all know that ye are my disciples, if ye have love one to another.
(John 13.34–35)

Proud Romans were heard to exclaim, 'Behold how [these Christians] love one another: and how they are ready to die for each other.'[3] Before long, Roman imperial persecution fell upon the followers of this new faith, testing them severely. Christians were tortured and slaughtered mercilessly. Many went to their deaths singing songs of divine praise.

In modern times, at Azusa Street, a different approach was taken. The white Pentecostals separated from their black brothers and sisters, compromising with the racial hatreds of the times. The racial separation of the Pentecostal movement meant that the Christian love uniting white and black Pentecostals no longer highlighted the movement. This compromise betrayed a sinful denial of the newly found love joining black and white Pentecostals together. This sinful separation has never been admitted as wrong, or confessed by the white separatists.

In our Holy Bible, we find a surprising episode of racial separation in the new Christian centre of Antioch, a racial separation between Jews and Gentiles. This separation of Christians was denounced in the strongest possible terms by the apostle Paul as a denial of the very gospel itself.

Following the martyrdom of Stephen in Jerusalem, many believers had fled for safety to the important Roman city of Antioch in the north, the imperial capital of Syria. A great many Gentiles joined the church of Antioch, making it the new centre of Christianity. It was the Christians of Antioch who sent Paul forth on his three missionary journeys. Indeed, it was at Antioch that the very name of the new faith, 'Christian', was first given: 'The disciples were called Christians first in Antioch' (Acts 11.26). There was no racial prejudice or separation among the Christians in Antioch. Indeed, their foremost leader was himself a black Christian from North Africa.

At Antioch, the episode of sinful racial separation cited in Scripture brought forth an almost bitter confrontation between Paul and Peter, the two leading apostles there. Paul and Barnabas had moved to Antioch to help its church leaders. All went well until a group of Jewish Christians sent by the apostle James arrived from Jerusalem. They refused to eat with Gentile Christians. Peter had been visiting before their arrival, eating freely with the many Gentile Christians. But when the Jerusalem group came and refused to eat with the Gentiles, Peter joined them, separating himself from the Gentiles. Paul reported that he withstood Peter to his face, regarding him as blameworthy because Peter 'walked not uprightly according to the truth of the gospel' (Galatians 2.11–14). Paul considered that Peter's approval of separating the races was behaviour not to be tolerated in a Christian church.

The Christian leaders at Antioch, prophets and teachers, were listed as 'Barnabas who was visiting there, Simeon that was called Niger, and Lucius of Cyrene, and Manaen, who had been brought up with Herod the tetrarch and Saul, later called Paul' (Acts 13.1). Note the inclusion of 'Simeon that was called Niger'. In the Latin language of Rome, the word 'Niger' (pronounced with either a hard or a soft 'g') means the colour black. So we have Simeon (or Simon) who was called the black man, a primary leader in Antioch praying, fasting, prophesying and teaching. He was the leader of those who prayed and laid hands on Saul and Barnabas, sending them forth as the first Christian missionary team in history (Acts 13.1–3). In other words Simeon was a black Christian man.

Simeon is the same man referred to as Simon of Cyrene, who was called upon to carry the cross of our Lord Jesus to his place of crucifixion (Matthew 27.32; Mark 15.21; Luke 23.26). One fateful day during the Jewish Passover observance, Simon of Cyrene, the black African, was visiting Jerusalem from the country. Simon came upon – or he may have been following – the crucifixion procession of our Lord, interested in the monumental drama he was unexpectedly witnessing.

Being in Jerusalem for Passover meant that Simon was already a devout believer in the chosen people of Israel, with their faith in the God of Abraham, Isaac and Jacob. He may well have heard of Jesus before leaving Africa, as a part of the large and ancient Jewish community there.

By one of the most remarkable divine providences ever recorded, our Lord falters while struggling to carry his cross and Simon of Cyrene is called upon by the Roman soldiers to take up the cross. Almighty God himself chose a beloved black man for the supremely great honour of carrying our Lord's cross. He thus becomes the chosen and elect father figure for all those black believers to come in future times.

When the Roman soldiers looked around for someone to carry our Lord's cross, and settled on Simon of Cyrene, the black African man, it is possible they were inclined to choose him because of his colour. It is more likely that Simon, beyond his colour, was a powerfully built man, showing great physical strength. The soldiers would have selected a man fully capable of carrying the cross all the way to the place of crucifixion. They would under no circumstances be eager to stop the procession yet again.

As Simon of Cyrene, the black man, took the bloodstained cross from the bleeding hands of our Lord, the sacred blood of Christ touched his own hands. Our suffering Lord, with the crown of thorns in place, is likely looking directly into the face of dear Simon as the cross is given to him. The sacred cross comes to rest on Simon's shoulder, within inches of his face. Our Lord himself begins walking again, only a few feet from Simon. A miracle is taking place in Simon's heart. During that last walk to Calvary, so intimately close to our Lord, Simon is being transformed. Not long after taking the cross, Simon would have heard our Lord's words to the women following the cross. It is likely that he was the one who reported them to the beloved physician, Luke, for his Gospel account (Luke 23.27–31).

Simon doubtless remained at the cross with our Lord until the very end. He saw the cruel nails piercing his hands and feet. He watched our Lord being lifted up. He gazed at the sign over the cross, 'JESUS OF NAZARETH THE KING OF THE JEWS . . . written in Hebrew, and Greek, and Latin' (John 19.19–21). He heard the mockeries of the passing crowds. He listened carefully to the seven immortal words our Lord spoke from the cross. He gave ear as our Lord requested forgiveness for all from the heavenly Father. He heard with awe as our Lord opened paradise for the dear condemned man on the cross next to him. He watched as the precious blood of redemption drained slowly from our Lord's body. The triumphant words of our Lord fell upon his ears, 'It is finished' (John 19.30).

He marvelled as the Roman soldiers gambled for the seamless robe of our Lord. He lived through the terrible darkness that fell over the earth for three full hours (Matthew 27.45). He heard our Lord commend his Spirit to the heavenly father. He beheld our Lord give up the last breath of life from his body. He gazed in horror as the Roman soldier thrust his spear through the divine side of our Lord. He felt the power of the earthquake. He marvelled at the wondrous words of the Roman centurion, 'Truly this was the Son of God' (Matthew 27.54). Finally, he might have helped Joseph of Arimathea and Nicodemus ever so lovingly take down the body of our Lord, and carefully lay it in the rich man's nearby tomb.

From the cross, our Lord probably looked upon Simon with heartfelt appreciation, and a wealth of loving kindnesses and tender mercies, given wordlessly. If so, this inexpressibly beautiful moment would go far to explain Simon's later leadership of the Christian centre in Antioch.

Following the historic Passover, Simon remained in the Holy Land. He was probably among the 120 gathered in the Upper Room awaiting the Holy Spirit. Later, we learn of him in the city of Antioch, the leader of a great centre of Christian faith second only to Jerusalem. It may well have been Simon who coined the new name, Christians, for the Antioch community of believers.

This remarkable story of Simon the black man, chosen by Almighty God to carry the cross of our Lord Jesus in his time of need, has been largely forgotten, or repressed. Historic works of art, films showing the crucifixion of Christ, and other illustrations of Simon, usually show him as a white man.

Please note carefully, Almighty God himself created Simon, ordained Simon, remembered Simon, guided Simon to be his special envoy to our weakening Lord at the very moment he faltered while carrying his cross. Almighty God himself appointed his beloved Simon of Cyrene, the black man, the man of colour, to be given the honour of partnering with our Lord Jesus to carry his cross for him to Calvary. No other follower of our Lord in all history has been so honoured as Simon of Cyrene, the black man, the man of colour. God himself joined the races together at the cross of Calvary. Are you able to appreciate how highly our heavenly Father honours and pays tribute not only to this divinely beloved black man, but to his precious long-suffering people of colour?

There is even more to the story of Simon, the black man from North Africa, who came by divine guidance to Jerusalem to fulfil his destiny in the very shadow of our Lord's cross. Later, after Simon has become the strong leader of the faithful believers in Antioch, he becomes even better known as the father of two outstanding Christian sons, the men of colour, Rufus and Alexander, who follow him as leaders of the new faith (Mark 15.21).

Rufus becomes prominent among the Christians in Rome (Romans 16.13). When our beloved brother Paul, the great apostle, is looking forward to visiting Rome, he writes ahead to the Roman Christians there. Paul mentions Rufus, paying high and affectionate tribute to him as among the very elect. High praise indeed.

By that time Simon, this African black man of spectacular Christian destiny, has passed from the scene. His widow, his beloved wife, is living in Rome with her son Rufus. This godly woman has endeared herself to Paul, the great apostle, as his own spiritual mother (Romans 16.13). Honours upon honours, among the first Christians, for our Lord's beloved people of colour. This divinely given lesson of racial togetherness has been largely overlooked today.

We have been considering Pentecostal spirituality, energized by some leading black Christians, in both ancient and modern times. Today we are said to be living in a postmodern world. Is the postmodernism of today a threat or an opportunity for Pentecostal spirituality? How does postmodernism have an impact on our belief and practice of spirituality? Can our theological education be more effective in meeting the challenges of a postmodern world?

The essence, or keynote, of postmodernism is a denial of the very concept of truth as Christians have known it. In the mindset attributed to postmodernism, there is no absolute truth possible; all truth is relative. According to this approach, there is no truth as we have known it in the past, no truth worthy of the name, no truth that is always true, in all places, for everyone, at all times, for ever. What is true for you may not be true for me, or for anyone.

Postmodernism, at its heart – if it has a heart – is a completely sceptical denial that there can be any truth given to humans by Almighty God himself. From the postmodernist perspective, it therefore follows that our historic Christian faith, and the Pentecostal spirituality based upon it, is passé, a relic from the outdated past, at best irrelevant in our time, something like dinosaurs.

Is this a challenge to us or a threat? Surely it is both. Make no mistake about it, this denial of truth as Christians have known truth, and proclaimed truth, over all our past centuries, and as our holy Scriptures present truth, is very challenging. This is a vicious, direct and deadly attack upon the very heart and soul of our Christian faith and Pentecostal spirituality. Our historic faith has always been one of truth that is divinely true, everywhere, at all times, always and for ever, as given by Almighty God himself.

The postmodern attack upon truth is an attack upon the sacred person of our Lord himself. He stated with great clarity, 'I am the way, the truth, and the life: no man cometh unto the Father but by me' (John 14.6). The truth of our historic faith is truth given to us by the immaculate, perfect, holy and sacred words of Almighty God himself. If the postmodern view of truth as relative prevails over our faith, it will, so to speak, crucify our blessed Lord and Saviour all over again. It would mean that he died in vain.

To meet the threats and challenges of postmodernism, we need to reaffirm and deepen our faith in the immaculate perfection of our divinely given holy Scriptures, the basis for all our spirituality and spiritual formation. The very heart and soul of our faith is the everlasting mission to present the saving truth of Almighty God to a world that is lost and dying without that truth.

Christians in every generation have given their lives for the faith that our Holy Bible presents in words of absolute truth. Among the very last dying words of the apostle Paul, it is written: 'All scripture is given by inspiration of God' (2 Timothy 3.16). That is to say, the words of our divinely given Holy Bible have been breathed into perfect being by the very breath of Almighty God, a precious, sacred gift from on high. This is the truth of Almighty God himself, fashioned into perfect human words, which to believe brings the priceless gift of eternal salvation, and deliverance from a world that is eternally lost and dying, with a death that is everlasting.

The viewpoint of postmodernism, that relative so-called truth is somehow new and up to date, more modern than modernity itself, is misleading and deceptive. Scepticism towards absolute truth is not something new at all. The sceptical view of truth has been well known since the very beginnings of ancient Greek philosophy, fully 800 years before the coming of Christ.

Such denial of absolute truth is found at the very heart of our sacred scriptures. When our beloved Lord Jesus was violently arrested by the Jewish religious authorities, during the full darkness of night time, and presented to the Roman governor, Pontius Pilate, for crucifixion, Pilate examined our Lord carefully.

Pilate had been appointed by the Roman emperor himself, and as such he was a wealthy Roman aristocrat, who would have had the finest education available at Rome. He was thoroughly familiar with the glories of ancient Greece, especially Greek philosophy, and the well-known sceptical view of truth.

During the Roman trial of our Lord, he was asked by Pilate, 'Are you the king of the Jews?' Our Lord answered, saying:

'My kingdom is not of this world: if my kingdom were of this world, then would my servants fight, that I should not be delivered to the Jews: but now is my kingdom not from hence.'

Pilate therefore said unto him, 'Art thou a king then?' Jesus answered him, 'Thou sayest that I am a king. To this end was I born, and *for this cause came I into this world, that I should bear witness to the truth. Every one that is of the truth heareth my voice.*

Pilate saith unto him [alas!!!], 'What is truth?'
(John 18.33, 36–38, emphasis and quotation marks added)

So, Pontius Pilate, with a dismissive swipe at the very idea of divinely given truth, taken directly from his education in sceptical Greek philosophy, turns away from the thought of any real truth worthy of the name. He ends the conversation, turning his back on our Lord. The great apostle Paul, brilliantly educated himself, clearly warns us against such sceptical philosophy, saying, 'Beware lest any man spoil you through philosophy and vain deceit, after the tradition of men, after the rudiments of the world, and not after Christ, for in him dwelled all the fullness of the Godhead bodily' (Colossians 2.8–9). What great, awesome truth we have been given by the Word of Almighty God himself. The divine words given to his people by Almighty God are more than sufficient to meet every threat, or challenge, from postmodernism.

There is said to be an ancient Chinese proverb, 'May you live in interesting times.' What times could possibly be more interesting, or challenging, than those in which the very heart and soul of our Christian faith and Pentecostal spirituality are under such widespread and continual attacks? To so attack the truth of our faith and spirituality is truly satanic, from the god of this world, so clearly described for us by our Lord in holy Scripture. These Scriptures leave no doubt that Satan, and all his deceptions, are doomed.

Could anyone who is devoted to our Lord and his truth wish for a greater challenge? Our holy Scriptures call us to rise up to the challenges of our times, stated so well long ago: 'Beloved . . . it was needful for me to write unto you . . . that ye should earnestly contend for the faith which was once delivered unto the saints' (Jude 3). Our mission today is to educate and train leaders dedicated to contending for our historic faith, amid every threat or challenge.

In our postmodern world, the challenge for Christian education is clear: to drink deeply from the fountain of apostolic truth, the truth of the holy Scriptures, to provide truth for our generation to overcome, with God's help, the challenges and threats of postmodern scepticism. The early Christians overcame the mighty Roman Empire with the power of their true faith. We are called to do no less today.

In this great struggle for the entitlement of Christian truth, black Pentecostal Christians have a hidden resource, the heritage of their historic slavery. Only nobility of soul could have enabled black slaves to embrace the faith professed by their slave masters, and yet find greater depths of understanding and love in that Christian faith than the professions of the slave masters. Out of those vast sufferings has come a capacity to truly love, in a Christ-like way, as our Lord commanded: 'This is my commandment, That ye love one another, as I have loved you. Greater love hath no man than this, that a man lay down his life for his friends. Ye are my friends, if ye do whatsoever I command you' (John 15.12–14).

Out of the great suffering of Christians who are black, is that remarkable depth of Pentecostal spirituality, an authentic Christian faith highlighted by genuine love. There is a depth of genuine love, a love that has suffered long, and a wealth of kindness afforded by the grace of God. Long suffering, with kindness, brings forth a love that is our Lord himself. From out of horrific suffering, our lord brings forth that Christ-like love he wishes for his people. This miraculous love has come from the depths of black Christian suffering, expressed with great kindness. It is the very definition of Christian love as written for us. 'Love suffers long, and is kind' (1 Corinthians 13.4).

In one of the great surprises of human history, the black slaves found in the words of holy Scripture a deeper depth of divine truth and divine love. They loved scriptures not usually noticed by the slave masters: 'He hath put down the mighty from their seats, and exalted them of low degree. He hath filled the hungry with good things; and the rich He hath sent empty away' (Luke 1.52–53). Again, 'Of a truth . . . God is no respecter of persons: but in every nation he that feareth Him, and worketh righteousness, is accepted with Him' (Acts 10.34–35). And again, 'He is despised and rejected of men; a man of sorrows, and acquainted with grief . . . and with His stripes we are healed' (Isaiah 53.3–5).

Out of this great black Christian slave faith has come a repertoire of some of the finest spiritual songs of all time, the Negro spirituals. My grandfather, who had a fine baritone voice, led Christian singing all his life. His favourite song was the spiritual, 'Swing low, sweet chariot, comin' for to carry me home'. There is no other music to compare with those great and deeply moving Christian slave songs.

W. E. B. Dubois wrote:

> The Negro folk-song – the rhythmic cry of the slave – stands today not simply as the sole American music, but as the most beautiful expression of human experience born this side of the seas. It has been neglected, it has been, and is, mistaken and misunderstood; but notwithstanding, it still remains as the singular spiritual heritage of the nation and the greatest gift of the Negro people. [4]

Consider the ways of divine providence. The ancient chosen people of Abraham, and our black Christian people of Western civilization, were both subjected to times of awful slavery. Our Lord God called the people of Abraham to be his chosen people. Then, strangely, he put them through more than 400 years of Egyptian slavery. Later, black Christians of the West came through slavery as well, a slavery even more cruel and devastating than the Egyptian slavery of ancient times.

Does not that fact of history tell you of a divinely given destiny for black Bible-believing Christians? There is a destiny, and a depth of believing faith, that can only come forth from the horrific suffering of human slavery. Both ancient Israel and our black community of today came through slavery, as by a divinely ordained providential plan. Our heavenly Father has redeemed both Israel and our modern-day black Christian community from their times of slavery to fulfil a purpose only possible through real suffering, accompanied by great kindness.

Deep in the very souls of black Christians, there is a genuine meekness and lowliness akin to the divine heart of Jesus himself.

In our New Testament there is only one mention of the divine heart of Jesus. Our Lord himself speaks of his divine heart, in terms of meekness and lowliness. He says,

Come unto me, all ye that labour and are heavy laden, and I will give you rest. Take my yoke upon you, and learn of me; for I am meek and lowly in heart: and ye shall find rest unto your souls. For my yoke is easy, and my burden is light. (Matthew 11.28–30)

The souls of black Christians bond with the very heart of Jesus in that meekness and lowliness. It is a lowliness of the highest order. Here is the glory hidden in the souls of black Christians, a quality from the very heart of Jesus himself.

One final thought. The scepticism of postmodernism has influenced very many theological faculties, seminaries and Christian education centres of today. The true words of holy Scripture are being presented as unreliable. There is a relatively new method of Bible study and analysis, coming historically from the theological faculties in Germany, called the method of higher criticism. This method is a sceptical way of reading the Holy Bible itself; the belief from this standpoint is that holy Scripture is unreliable.

This method of theological education reduces our Holy Bible to an ordinary book, to be criticized, corrected or denied. In this process, the human being passes judgement upon the Bible, instead of allowing the Bible to pass judgement upon the human being. The Bible is searched for all manner of supposed errors, mistakes, fabrications, erroneous beliefs and the like. By this method, we are told that Isaiah did not write the book of Isaiah, as stated in the Bible. The apostle Paul did not write most of his epistles, as previously reported. And on and on and on. In the extreme form of this method, some 90 per cent of our Lord's own words are considered to have been reported falsely.

This method usually goes hand in hand with a sceptical denial of all supernatural elements in our Holy Bible. Therefore, narratives describing the virgin birth of our Lord, the voice of Almighty God from heaven, the bodily resurrection and ascension of our Lord, and others, are considered to be untrue.

Long ago, the apostle Peter gave the people of God the answer to such scepticism when he referred to the Transfiguration:

> we have not followed cunningly devised fables, when we made known unto you the power and coming of our Lord Jesus Christ, but were eyewitnesses of his majesty. For he received from God the Father honour and glory, when there came such a voice to him from the excellent glory, This is my beloved son, in whom I am well pleased. And this voice which came from heaven we heard, when we were with him in the holy mount.
> (2 Peter 1.16–18)

Today, the sceptical line of attack associated with methods of higher criticism is being widely used. Our Lord himself said that the Scriptures cannot be broken (Matthew 5.17–18; John 10.35). But this new method of Bible criticism breaks it into many pieces. The entire dimension of 'the holy' disappears from the Holy Bible by this method of education. What can possibly remain of the gospel itself, and the awesome majesty of Almighty God, if the words of our Holy Bible are deemed to be so unreliable? It is no wonder that many theological seminaries and church pulpits today are not proclaiming the gospel at all.

Thankfully, our faithful Lord, who has promised never, ever to leave us or forsake us (Hebrews 13.5), stands ready to guide his teachers to a better, deeper, more truthful understanding of our Holy Bible than that found in such a cynical approach to Bible study. Our Lord Jesus spoke of the perfect truth, even of every jot and tittle, of the Old Testament in the Hebrew language (Hebrews 5.18).

As our world moves ever closer to the prophesied last days of earth as we know it, there is foretold to be much falling away, apostasy in the churches, a deliberate rejection of the revealed truth clearly given in holy Scripture. The visible churches will fall more and more into apostasy, with many professing belief, 'Having a form of godliness, but denying the power thereof . . . Ever learning, and never able to come to the knowledge of the truth . . . so do these also resist the truth' (2 Timothy 3.5, 7, 8). The predicted future of the visible Church is apostasy and judgement.

But within that visible Church, lives, and there will continue to live, a holy remnant, the true Church, known to God alone, elect, and faithful (Hebrews 12.23; Luke 18.6–8). The future destiny of this hidden and true Church is glory.

Our mission is to be faithful to the faith once delivered to the saints who were with our Lord Jesus from the beginning, and to the words that transmit that faith to us. The mission of Christian education is to carry forward the apostolic faith, the faith once delivered to the saints, fully expressed and explained in an inspired Holy Bible, given to us by Almighty God himself.

Let me close with this: our Lord Jesus has two favourite words. First, he says 'come', as in 'Come unto me' (Matthew 11.28). Let us ever be coming to him, in prayer, worship, praise, adoration, Holy Communion, to draw strength for the challenges of our times. Second, he says 'go', as in 'Go ye into all the world, and preach the gospel to every creature' (Mark 16.15). As believers, let us ever be coming to him, and going for him, faithfully, until he comes again.

## Notes

1 D. J. Nelson, "'For Such a Time as This": The story of Bishop William J. Seymour and the Azusa Street Revival', PhD dissertation, University of Birmingham, May 1981, pp. 37, 75.
2 A. H. Anderson, *An Introduction to Pentecostalism* (Cambridge: Cambridge University Press, 2014, p. 3.
3 Tertullian, *Apology*, trans. S. Thelwall, ch. 39, <https://www.logos library.org/tertullian/apology/39.html>, accessed 28 January 2020.
4 W. E. B. Dubois, *The Souls of Black Folk* (New York: New American Library, 1969), p. 265.

# 3

# Pentecostalism, politics and justice[*]

## STEVEN LAND

The global Pentecostal movement is rich and very diverse in its cultural settings and structure, of mission, worship and discipling. But it is almost completely derived from the eighteenth-century Methodist and nineteenth-century Holiness movements.[1] By sheer force of numbers, Pentecostal churches are having a huge impact as they interact with, transform and accommodate various cultures. They are struggling to discern the world (1 John 2.15–16) in the culture while engaging more and more in compassionate care ministries in several community developments. They have their own non-Marxist version of liberation theology in the Spirit for social action. These churches are embodying the meaning of the kingdom as they participate in the state and its socio-economic programmes as the community of believers. There is tension between the Church and the world, especially as socio-economic fortunes improve. No longer just the 'vision of the disinherited', Pentecostals are pressing into uncharted territory while seeking to avoid being used by political parties and other factions.

---

[*] This chapter is a revision of the original lecture delivered by Steven J. Land at the 2016 Oliver Lyseight Lecture Series. The editorial work was completed by David Sang-Ehil Han with the author's permission.

A reconsideration and expansion of the doctrine of holiness is beginning to emerge among Pentecostals and other evangelicals. Triune holiness is seen as having a structure of righteousness, a content of divine love, and a dynamic eschatological power that drives all things to the consummation of the kingdom of God. God as eschatological presence calls Pentecostals to live responsively from that presence and to be a part of an eschatological missionary fellowship. Neither man-made utopia nor individual piety captures the dynamic of the overarching, already present, not-yet-consummated kingdom reign of God. This reign, at the very least, requires us to respond to those of our neighbours who are in need of justice, love and empowerment and also, with our neighbours, to care for creation with responsible stewardship.

In the following pages, we will seek to provide an overview of how modern Pentecostalism can discuss and develop the heart of an original, mature vision while engaging in its comprehensive mission of social holiness in the power of the Spirit.

# Challenges and choices

Paul exhorts the Ephesians to 'walk worthy of the [calling] . . . with all lowliness and meekness, with longsuffering, forbearing one another in love' since they were called in 'one body . . . one Spirit . . . one hope . . . one Lord . . . one faith, one baptism; one God and Father of all, who is above all, and through all, and in you all' (Ephesians 4.1–6). If indeed there is only one God, then there can be only one true faith corresponding to the revelation of the one true Lord. Additionally, the ultimate purpose and mission of our lives must come to terms with the mission and purpose of this one true God. God has revealed himself in Jesus Christ who, by the power of the Holy Spirit, offered himself as a sacrifice for our sins, once and for all.

Even though recent religious surveys tend to indicate that the number of those whose religious preference is 'none' keeps rising in the global north,[2] religion continues to multiply unabated throughout the rest of the world – especially in Latin America, Africa and Asia.[3] Of more than seven billion people on Planet Earth, over one third profess Christianity. We cannot assume that they are all serving the triune God of Scripture. All the thousands of religions of the world present many 'gods' and their correlated 'salvations'. The northern hemisphere of the globe is characterized by a continuing powerful, integrated secularization of every facet of life in modern society. Since religion is at the heart of culture, we may expect more conflicts as civilizations clash and cause more individuals to suffer serious doubt as people in modern society become overwhelmed by the tidal waves of conformation, propaganda and hyper-modern (postmodern) higher education. The Church, especially in the northern hemisphere, must make choices: whether to be a group of holy covenantal, unified congregations or contractual spiritual enterprises; ministers of generous congregations or magicians with a paying clientele; biblical disciples or social 'winners'; servants or celebrities; faithful or merely famous. They must choose between knowing the sheep and merely counting them, between biblical doctrines and easily marketed slogans – bumper sticker doctrines such as 'once saved, always saved', between deep moral convictions and merely suggested guidelines, between a spirituality for all of life and fragmented thrilling experiences, between a formative historical process with God and the Church and merely entertaining events. Choices matter.

Pentecostals in particular must decide whether to try to maintain a few Pentecostal distinctions of style or live out a distinctive Pentecostal way of life in the Spirit. Will we have collaborative interdependence or adversarial independence? Do we want generic secular styles of leadership for the Church or leaders who undergo a distinctive Pentecostal process with a Pentecostal result? Will we still seek to proclaim and live out the 'full gospel' or merely embrace alternative principles for self-improvement?

Will we be a 'contrast culture', completely separated unto the Lord, or just another culturally assimilated private organization, waiting for someone to yank our financial support unless we compromise our faith? All these enquiries seem mild when we consider the fact that some Christians in other parts of the world are undergoing horrific persecution; however, too often our experiences and expressions of spiritual life are distorted or poorly developed.

For example, when justification and sanctification are fragmented, we can see the drift towards justification of sin and not that of the sinner. Wilful sinning is never justified (Heb. 10.28–31). Justification from God has as its goal our declaration for his righteousness. Spirit-baptism, unless coupled with a healthy emphasis on sanctification, often leads to presumptive leadership in ministry and, consequently, becomes a source of personal achievement and enfranchisement rather than an occasion to deepen the spirit of humility and gratitude for the gift given. We contradict our claims of maturity and Spirit-filling when we show no fear of God, when we profane (take in vain) his name. Think of how frequently we hear 'God' or 'Jesus' used as slang by adults and children, spoken as a profane epithet – Christians included. We cannot be Spirit-filled while sinning against the Holy Spirit in the following ways: grieving the Spirit (Ephesians 4.30), quenching the Spirit (1 Thessalonians 5.19), resisting the Spirit (Acts 7.51), insulting the Spirit (Hebrews 10.26–29), lying to the Spirit (Acts 5.1–11) and blaspheming the Spirit (Matthew 12.31–34).

When we become overly familiar, irreverent and casual with the things of God, we begin to ease into these sins. When we put ourselves, someone else or things of this world at the centre of our lives, we become skewed and spiritually imbalanced. Dorotheos of Gaza, a sixth-century monk, admonishes us to think of God as the centre of our lives and all creation.[4] Moving towards the centre would then mean becoming more intimate with God and one another. There can only be one centre. We must prayerfully re-centre our lives, families and churches on the triune God, who can hold and produce moral integrity in our lives.

There is the one true God, who alone is the Creator, the Redeemer and the Sustainer of life. This one God, who ordered the heavens by his laws of design and purpose and complexity, also orders our lives according to his precepts and laws which, like him, are holy, just and good. His character, not ours, is the ultimate standard for all we desire, decide and do. There is only one Lord and Saviour, and that is Jesus Christ. The Holy Spirit bears witness only to Jesus Christ and his gospel. No other saviour, no other Spirit and no other gospel. Scripture also teaches us that there is only one Spirit who leads, comforts, illuminates, inspires, convicts, empowers and shows us things to come. The Holy Spirit of God bears witness to Jesus Christ and not to himself. He alone can help us fathom the truths of God while also discerning the seducing spirits and lying wonders in the world.

The Father, the Son and the Holy Spirit are therefore triune persons whose individual identities are constituted by their inner relationships. We live, however, in a society where people deny Christ instead of themselves and become isolated individuals, bound and blinded in a private hell of darkness, distortion, degradation and depraved indifference to God's justice and judgement. Recovering the 'Triune centre', that is, God at the centre becomes a crucial necessity for believers whose journeys in the world are filled with challenges that place them on the crossroads of making choices. There is one Lord, one faith and one mission, being carried out by this missionary God and all who participate in his life and love his presence.

# The faith and the faithful

We live in a day when people, including Christians, do not so much despise sound doctrine as remain indifferent to it; they believe that it has nothing to do with the reality of their daily lives. According to them, 'doctrine' represents nothing more than a set of ideas constructed to control others or calm their fears of the unknown or the uncertainties of life. It is not a lot different than in Paul's day, when he had to exhort Timothy concerning the doctrinal task of a pastor. So, in 1 and 2 Timothy, Paul tells Timothy:

- Command them not to teach strange (non-biblical) doctrines or give heed to speculations that cause useless disputes rather than godly edification (1 Timothy 1.3, 4). The purpose of the command is love from a pure heart, a good conscience and sincere faith (1 Timothy 1.5).
- Use the law 'lawfully', not to 'justify' but to 'direct' a moral life. Christians are neither legalists nor libertines; the law is provided to help guide and direct the ungodly and lawless (1 Timothy 1.8–11).
- As Paul admonishes Timothy, Christians are to wage good warfare, holding on to faith and a good conscience (1 Timothy 1.18–20).
- We are to preach in faith and truth about Christ (1 Timothy 2.5–7).
- A bishop must be able (apt) to teach (1 Timothy 3.2).
- Deacons must hold the mystery of the faith in a pure conscience (1 Timothy 3.9).
- We are to be nourished in the words of faith and good doctrine (1 Timothy 4.6).
- We are to give attention to reading, exhortation and doctrine (1 Timothy 4.13).
- We are to withdraw from, and reject, those who do not

consent to wholesome words, those of Jesus Christ, and doctrine that conforms to godliness (1 Timothy 6.3–5).

- Guarding the sound doctrine entrusted to us, we are to avoid worldly and empty chatter and contradictions of false knowledge (1 Timothy 6.20–21).
- As Paul reminds Timothy, we are to hold fast to the exemplary witnesses of the faithful inherited and stay in the Scriptures – especially those that give doctrinal, moral guidance – in order to equip ourselves thoroughly to perform every good work (2 Timothy 3.10–17).
- We are to keep the goal in mind and fight the good fight, finishing the race while keeping the faith (2 Timothy 4.7).

As Paul instructs Timothy about the pastoral task with regard to teaching sound doctrine, we should bear in mind that the biblical faith of historical revelation and teaching has been entrusted to us, so that we may remember it faithfully in the present and pass it on to the next generation for the future. Hence, a major part of the Church's ministry is faithful preaching and teaching of the Word in the context of each new generation, labouring at the interface of theology and life.

There are, of course, many families in the global church of the living God. There is no such thing as a generic Christian church. Think of the often-heard remark that a church just wants to be like the New Testament church. To which we honestly reply: 'Which one?' – Corinth, Ephesus, Smyrna, Pergamum, Thyatira, Sardis, Philadelphia, Laodicea? That is, there are those whom we consider to be authentic Christians, although they may present the gospel of Jesus Christ with unique emphases and teachings of their own, which vary from those of other churches without the difference (or variance) being so critical or substantial as to remove them from a Christian fellowship; included in the examples of difference are modes of baptism (pouring, immersion, not at all), polity (episcopal, presbyterial, congregational) and tribulation teachings.

# The Wesleyan-Holiness Pentecostal perspective

When we review the historical and theological roots of the modern Pentecostal movements around the turn of the twentieth century, they are clearly marked, with particular emphases and teachings. Revisiting the historical and theological roots of Pentecostalism is of critical significance in faithfully remembering and transmitting our own distinctive identity in Christ.[5] For Pentecostals, when we are unclear about our 'full gospel' identity, when we are lax in training our ministers, and when we fail to disciple new members and our children, we drift away from our own faith foundation and look for someone else's ready-made identity in order to graft it on to our own. As a result, what we claim to believe and how we practise in ministry become disconnected and confused.

One example of this is the recent interest in Calvinism as a way to bring assurance and peace in the face of much that seems out of control and tragic in our world. What follows will be an example of how we might honour, but respectfully disagree with, another part of the family of God and continue to offer faithful teaching concerning the fullness of the Christian life from our Wesleyan-Holiness Pentecostal perspective. By this perspective we mean that there is an emphasis on the Christian life as a 'journey' (a 'way') in all the light of the written Word of God with wholehearted love and remaining filled with the Spirit.

To begin with, we should observe the historical and theological connection among the Wesleyan, the Holiness and the Pentecostal movements. The Wesleyan 'heart' movement of the eighteenth century became the Holiness revival of the nineteenth century and the Pentecostal renewal of the twentieth century, which has now renewed and touched every facet of the body of Christ and has ushered in the mightiest, most explosive missionary impact in the history of the Church. The theological heritage embedded in the modern Pentecostal movements then reaches back to the eighteenth century and, through Wesley, to the churches of the West and the East, all the way back to the biblical era.

In this vein, we should observe that most if not all of the early Pentecostals insisted that Christian perfection or entire sanctification preceded Spirit-baptism. Even non-Wesleyans in the nineteenth century (e.g. the Oberlin and Keswick movements) were 'wesleyanized' (and thus 'arminianized'). The Holiness movement was also the cradle of Pentecostalism. In 1983, Donald Wheelock, in his doctoral dissertation, concluded that Pentecostals are in agreement that 'personal holiness precedes Spirit-Baptism, whether that holiness is understood as a crisis experience in which the root of inbred sin is plucked up, or a victorious consecration which is maintained and deepened by the assistance of the Holy Spirit.'[6] This was the position of William Seymour in the Azusa Street revival. Even though in the past, for various reasons, there have been intense conflicts between Holiness and Pentecostal churches, this was to a large extent a family dispute between fraternal, if not identical, twins. Melvin Dieter in his landmark book, *The Holiness Revival of the Nineteenth Century*, noted that even the largest and more 'baptistic' Pentecostal body, the Assemblies of God, has a spiritual dynamic that is at least equally derived from a meeting between the historical camp and advocates of perfectionism.[7]

It is significant to note that the Holiness connection in this regard carries with it the nineteenth-century concern for abolition, prohibition, women's ministry and rights, and societal reform according to the righteous standards of God. In other words, Holiness is never understood as an interiorization of spiritual experiences but is rather layered with both the personal and the social dimensions. The 'inward turning' towards God in love is necessarily correlated with one's 'outward demonstration'

61

of that love in actions that speak of God's justice and righteousness in life.

But when Pentecostalism and the Holiness churches in the USA and elsewhere were adversely affected by the aftermath of the Civil War, Reconstruction, the new higher criticism of the Bible, the liberal social gospel and the increasing upward mobility of Methodism, they were forced to choose between fundamentalism and modernism. Choosing fundamentalism blunted the quest for personal and social holiness and restricted it much more to direct personal relief efforts. Both movements (Holiness-Pentecostals and fundamentalists) were present at the founding of the National Association for Evangelicals (NAE) in the 1940s, despite the fact that in North America the word 'evangelical' has, in the past, more often than not excluded or redefined the Holiness-Pentecostal paradigm in favour of the more Presbyterian-Fundamentalist paradigm. Wesleyan-Holiness Pentecostal identity would be greatly impoverished if it lost or ignored its Wesleyan roots, because it is that connection that can be traced back, east and west, to claim the full Christian heritage of the church.

# Dialogue, dissent and collaboration

Pentecostals can also be enriched by the Calvinist and Reformed heritage of the Church. Alongside Calvin, Pentecostals confess belief in a triune holy God, who is the Creator, Redeemer and Sustainer. The infinite God has accommodated himself to us finite human beings by giving the Scriptures and displaying the wonders of creation. For Calvin, the Christian life is one of real spiritual progress through a lifelong process of mortification and vivification. On our way to hell or heaven (and the new creation), we acknowledge with Calvin the so-called third use of the moral law of God to guide ethical Christian living and endeavour. There is rich discussion of the person and work of the Spirit in Calvin and the modern reformed Charismatic movement. By the Spirit, believers can taste divinity in the Scriptures and be enlightened and taught to understand and apply the Word in daily living. All the blessings of salvation and life are the result of the grace of Christ, and all have their meritorious base in the sacrifice of Christ. These things and many more Pentecostals share with their Calvinist brothers and sisters. With them, we confess and teach salvation by grace through faith. Though there are many shades and branches of Calvinism today (as there are of Pentecostalism), the focus here will be on the Calvinism represented by the classical five points of the proverbial 'TULIP': total depravity, unconditional election, limited atonement, irresistible grace and the perseverance of the saints. Both Wesley and Calvin wrote much about sin.[8] To evidence this, Wesley wrote his longest treatise on the doctrine of sin. At the end, he agreed with Calvin that sin has affected every dimension of our existence. People created in God's image for love and fellowship have fallen and now are in a 'natural' state full of evil. But for John Wesley, no one was left in a totally natural state.[9]

For Calvin, 'common grace' was extended to fallen humanity, and this was the source of any goodness, truth or beauty in this world. This grace did not intend salvation. But for Wesley, God extended prevenient grace, which goes before justifying grace and intends salvation. Prevenient grace comes through the Christ who convicts everyone who comes into the world, through the revealing and enlightening activity of the Holy Spirit. These actions of Christ and the Holy Spirit account for the existence of conscience, a supernatural and not merely sociological reality. Prevenient grace also results in a measure of free will that enables us to receive and appropriate the blessings of God.[10] Because of this measure of freedom, humans are responsible for their actions, since in a merely natural state they would be filled with devils and only, always practise evil.

For both Calvin and Wesley, humans are unable to save themselves and have no natural free will. So, for Calvin, how is it possible to be saved? His answer is unconditional particular election, taking nothing into account in the person. God before creation and in his love and grace, with no necessity, chooses certain people to be saved. The corollary of this is unconditional particular reprobation. You cannot have one without the other. God passes over all those not elected to salvation and withholds saving grace from them. God not only foresaw that Adam would fall, he ordained it. God foresees nothing but what he decreed. And his decree precedes foreknowledge. Just as he gives salvation to the elect by working efficaciously in them, so through preaching the gospel he 'blinds and stupefies reprobates whom he created to perish eternally'. He calls them 'that they may be more deaf; he kindles a light that they may be more blind; He brings his doctrine to them, that they may be more ignorant; and applies His remedy to them, that they may not be healed.[11]

For Wesley, God decreed in the beginning to choose in Christ all who believe unto salvation. Such a decree proceeds from his goodness and not that of the creature. And God, from the beginning, decreed to reprobate all who stubbornly and rebelliously continue in unbelief.[12] Christ died for all, and God desires all to be saved! For Calvin, on the other hand, multitudes were created to 'live a reproach and die everlastingly'.[13] Even common grace is actually damning grace. Wesley concluded, 'it was given, not to convert thee, but only to convince; not to make thee without sin, but without excuse; not to destroy, but to arm the worm that never dieth and to blow up the fire that never shall be quenched'.[14]

It follows in Calvin's system that those who are totally corrupt can and must be saved only by the unconditional election of God. Thus, Christ dies for all the elect and his blood is applied to and efficacious in only them. The Holy Spirit then works irresistibly and they are given justification, faith and forgiveness – all the blessings of salvation. The foundation of all such heart religion is the justification in the blood of Christ. But, whereas Wesley agrees with Calvin that Christ's blood is the only meritorious cause of salvation, he is appalled to find that the faith which works through love is being assaulted by the teaching that the imputation of Christ's righteousness excuses one from hungering and thirsting after righteousness. Desiring an inherent (imparted) righteousness is falsely equated with renouncing Christ, and those who preach inherent righteousness (that is, we become the righteousness of God in him) are being characterized as legalistic preachers ignorant of the gospel. Certain 'grace teachers' today propagate that faith, love, law, obedience, and works are all a multiple choice test, when in fact all have their scriptural place. We should recapture the words of John Wesley in this regard:

> [T]his is indeed 'a blow at the root', the root of all religion. Hereby, Christ is stabbed in the house of His friends . . . (and) the whole design of His death, namely to destroy the works of the devil, has been overthrown at a stroke. For wherever this doctrine is cordially received, it leaves no place for holiness. It demolishes it from top to bottom; it destroys both root and branch . . . here is the masterpiece of Satan: farther than this he cannot go. Men are holy without a grain of holiness in them; holy in Christ, however unholy in themselves; they are in Christ without one jot of the mind that was in Christ; though their nature is whole in them. They are 'complete in him', though they are in themselves as proud, vain, as covetous, and as passionate as ever. It is enough: they may be unrighteous still, seeing Christ has 'fulfilled all righteousness'.[15]

If believers reject, or turn away from, the possibility that God can create a clean heart, renew a right spirit and establish pure love to reign in the heart as the essence of entire sanctification, they end up accepting some compromised ideal with resignation replacing the aspiration and longing to be like Christ. That is, thinking that our sinful inclination is attached to, or drives, every act we carry out, believers falsely conclude: 'Why strive to be like Christ?'

But humanity was created for the triune God of love, for love and fellowship with God and others. With regard to God's love and sovereignty, Calvin sees God's love in terms of sovereignty and Wesley interprets God's sovereignty in terms of love.[16] Saving grace as love is independent of merit, achievement or endeavour. This grace is 'free for all and in all'. It is not limited by divine decrees which lead to fatalism, complacency or despair. Because salvation envisaged in this way is deeply relational, believers may defect and finally be unfaithful. This fact is underscored by considering the personal nature of sins against the Holy Spirit. The Holy Spirit may be resisted (Acts 7.51), quenched (1 Thessalonians 5.19) and grieved (Ephesians 4.30), insulted (Hebrews 10.26–29), lied to (Acts 5.1–11) and finally blasphemed (Matthew 12.31). God can deliver us from all our foes, but we can be deceived by the deceitfulness of sin and develop hearts hardened by unbelief. There are no major branches of Pentecostalism that have not been Arminian with regard to the perseverance of the saints. Eternal security was even rejected by one of the most prominent Baptist exegetes of the early twentieth century, Dale Moody.[17]

Pentecostals weep and travail in prayer over the lost and perishing. There is no heartless resting upon a divine decree or resignation: 'Whatever will be, will be.' Instead, there is a sharing in the passion and suffering of Christ that all may know him. Being full of the Holy Spirit does not mean that we leave behind the fellowship of his suffering or the conformity to the likeness of his death. For Pentecostals, a normal Christian life is marked by the fullness of the Spirit and has a cruciform shape.

Like other believers in the Protestant tradition, Pentecostals believe in justification by faith alone. However, for Pentecostals, this faith is never alone! It is the faith that, by the Holy Spirit, works through love. As William Seymour said more than a hundred years ago at Azusa Street, the fire of the Holy Spirit falls upon sacrifice. The greater the consecration, the greater the power, and this power is power to love righteously. Unless, and until, we recover this sense of 'praying through' and loving with a heart in which love reigns, we will continue to pursue the merely spectacular and the politically correct while missing the ever new and wonderful.

Wesleyan-Holiness Pentecostals embrace a discipleship of walking in the light of all Scripture, and of wholehearted pure love by the power of the Holy Spirit, who desires to fill all believers. God has decreed that all who believe unto salvation will be saved and that all who persist in unbelief will be damned. In keeping with the Wesleyan-Holiness Pentecostal vision, we must therefore take into account true virtue and not merely numbers. Big or small churches are not the point; faithfulness is the point. It is not how many we count; it is how many for whom we watch and care for their souls. Our worship must not be a mere spectacular event but part of a faith journey together, as believers experiencing Jesus in the Spirit – Jesus the Saviour, Jesus the Sanctifier, Jesus the Spirit-Baptizer, Jesus the Healer, and Jesus the Soon-coming King.

# The 'full gospel' in the Pentecostal tradition

At the beginning of the modern Pentecostal movements, the so-called 'full gospel' was often identified in terms of the above 'five-fold' dimensions of the gospel of Jesus. That is, Jesus who saves subsequently sanctifies and baptizes believers with the Spirit while demonstrating his atonement power through healing; furthermore, the salvation journey so portrayed has in view an urgent expectation of the eschatological reign of Jesus the King, who has promised to return. It should be noted, however, that the five-fold testimony that occurred in the beginning of the Pentecostal movement was not an attempt to limit the faith to only five points (as some have done with Calvinism), but to offer a dynamic shorthand way of registering the heart of the renewal and restoration, and to provide a lens through which to view the whole of Scripture and the Christian life and mission. It was centred in Christ, not the Holy Spirit or even the experience of the Spirit-baptism. Just as in the New Testament, the way of salvation was through the transforming work of God's grace, which testifies of the saving grace of Jesus Christ, the empowering presence of the Holy Spirit and the love of the Father for the world. With regard to the full or five-fold gospel today, we may note the following details about Jesus as Saviour, Sanctifier, Healer, Spirit-Baptizer and Soon-coming, Reigning King.[18]

## Jesus as Saviour

Salvation has often become 'easy-believism' – a call to repent and receive salvation with a grace/forgiveness announced for all sins past, present and future whether repented or not. This is a crossless gospel. On the contrary, having been brought into the family of God, believers are expected to journey in the way of salvation as those belonging to the Light (1 John 1).

## Jesus as Sanctifier

This has become forgiveness and growth (at our own pace) with no call to mortification of deeds of the flesh or filling with the love of God. It seems that many no longer know how to give an altar call or report of entire sanctification and full devotion. General growth has displaced a call to radical cleansing and love that drives out sinful desires, resistances and besetting sins. A compromised ideal has replaced a godly aspiration that groans after the fullness of joy which accompanies wholehearted love. Proceeding from initial sanctification when joined to Christ in regeneration (the Spirit's baptism of the believer into Christ), we ought to grow towards entire sanctification (fully consecrated and disposed, in moral integrity, to love and not lust), abiding and growing in Christ's infinite goodness, wisdom and knowledge for ever.

## Jesus as Healer

It seems the whole Pentecostal movement has been affected by the 'name it, claim it' word of faith. But this is not faith. A 'name it, claim it' theology is based on a total misunderstanding of 'binding' and 'loosing' in Matthew 16.19. We are to bind on earth what 'shall have been' bound or loosed in heaven based on what God requires or permits. So much of this seems designed for magicians who are seemingly masters of technique and propaganda, not shepherds or accountable teachers. So many seem skilled at moving crowds who love the spectacular but are being kept from the wonderful holy presence of God. Too many refuse to weep with those who weep. We continue to believe in and see miracles of all kinds, but signs should follow, not precede, believers. Jesus, who did many wonder-works, never advertised miracle services. When he twice fed the multitudes fish and bread and they returned a third time, the menu became his body and blood, and multitudes went away. The one true faith in Jesus must be advanced in humble ministry that recognizes the sovereignty and the faithfulness of God.

## Jesus as Spirit-Baptizer

As a result of losing our distinctive of Wesleyan sanctification, we often conflate love and power, or power and maturity. We are not more mature than other Christians who do not claim the experience of Spirit-baptism. We are simply better than we would have ever been if we had not been filled. When we are fully engaged in spiritual warfare, we will not ask if some have to be Spirit-filled, have to speak in tongues, or anything else God has for us. When we pray with words grounded in Scripture, when our prayers are identified with the groaning and sighs in the heart of God who so loved the world, and when we pray in one Spirit with words taught by the Spirit, our prayers will be more effective and discerning of the spirits operating in the world. Concurrently, we will also be able to discern the edifying encryption of the Holy Spirit as our spirit prays. So one must not teach others to speak in tongues. That is the work of the sovereign Holy Spirit who let the disciples tarry for days before filling them, on the one hand, while filling the household of Cornelius in one service, on the other.

## Jesus as Soon-coming, Reigning King

The kingdom of God is already inaugurated but not yet consummated. To the extent that we pray in the Spirit, we long for his appearing. Prayer is our highest privilege and deepest responsibility. 'Pray without ceasing' (1 Thessalonians 5.19) is a summons to become a prayer-full person and enter into the suffering of Christ with others. Prayerful reading of Scripture is the foundation of the truly spiritual life.

In our journey of salvation attending to the 'full gospel', we must not despise the Church and love the kingdom. The King of the kingdom is the head of the Church which is his body. The Church is the home of the strong and the weak, the sincere and the hypocrite, the carnal and the spiritual. But the Church is where we press towards the consummation while awaiting his reign in all the earth. The care for the Church in prayer, love, training and giving is the index of our care as the family of God. We are harbingers, forerunners of the kingdom, but we run together in the fellowship of the Church, endeavouring to leave no one behind on the field of battle. There is no salvation outside the body of Christ and there is not a true church that is not a missionary fellowship. We are called to the character of Christ in 'one body, Spirit, hope, Lord, faith, baptism'. This unity binds us inwardly and outwardly. Our hearts are knit together in love (Colossians 2.2) by the Holy Spirit, and outwardly we are on a mission, journeying together. There are two testaments, but one Bible. We are many, but we are one in the love of the God who is love.

The unity in Christ does not, however, negate propagation of our own distinctives of faith as Pentecostals. Catholics are characterized not just by a Catholic distinctive. The whole of their treatment of doctrine is affected by their theological commitment to the teaching of sacramental grace, Jesus being the quintessential sacrament of God. Lutherans are known to see the Christian faith from the standpoint of being simultaneously justified and sinners at the cross. Baptists generally embrace believer's baptism, congregational polity and eternal security, and all these doctrines and practices together constitute a whole (or 'gestalt'). Therefore, if Pentecostalism does not consist in one or two distinctives but is itself a whole, intelligible Christian family, how shall its distinctive way of being Christian be characterized?

Pentecostals live in response to the triune presence of God. Our view of the Christian life emphasizes a participation in the mission of God, no matter what our individual giftings might be. This is the death of nominal church membership and the emergence of a more 'church militant' approach in which every believer is called upon to be a Christ-like witness (in word, deed and character) to Jesus Christ in the power of the Spirit. For Pentecostals, the Bible is the Spirit-Word that lives in us and shines from us. We are to walk in all its light. What is our ultimate creed? If it's in the Bible, we believe it. If it is not there, we are not going to worry much about it, or shouldn't. When so many churches are defecting from God's Church and betraying Christ, calling evil good and good evil, when we are in perilous times of unprecedented mission impact, we must renew, restore, and foment spiritual revolution with all those who are called to wholehearted service. We need people to don the whole armour of faith and not sit down while others struggle and suffer. There ought to be more honour for true soldiers of the cross than any other soldiers. Eternal 'life and death' matters are at stake now, with a great ingathering and a great falling away.

# A comprehensive call

Once we are clear on the one true, triune God, and are ready to contend for the apostolic faith given in holy Scripture, and are convinced that Scripture is an infallible guide (by the Holy Spirit) which will equip us for all good works, we still need to understand what it means to be called. Mistakes are often made, however, as the meaning of the call gets fragmented. We have talked with other evangelicals about a call to repent, a call to disciple and a call to witness. In reality, however, these calls (in a manner analogous to the unity of the Trinity) are really one call. The call to repentance and faith is also simultaneously a call to discipleship and witness. To see it otherwise seems to present a Christ who invites us to repent so we will 'fly when we die and not fry' but adds discipleship only in the small print. Try getting new converts to take more time than a worship service or occasional class, or tell them you would love them to consider discipleship training for new converts. They would wonder if this is what they signed on to when they made their 'one time decision for Christ'. What often goes missing is our sense of being bought by Christ, belonging to him, and being at his disposal according to his timetable. We must first repent of our selfish view which causes us to deny Christ and not ourselves.

After we truly turn away from the world (that is, once we repent), we hear concurrently a call to be his disciples. It was none other than Jesus who commissioned the Church to go into all the world, making disciples and baptizing them in the name of the Father, Son and Holy Spirit. We are called, as his disciples, to be fully immersed in the life and mission of the triune God while obeying all that Jesus had commanded. We see this in particular in Matthew 16.24 where Jesus issues the call for discipleship. In issuing that call, Jesus commands as follows: 'If [anyone] will come after me, let him deny himself, and take up his cross and follow me.' Once a believer acknowledges the call to be his disciple, she acknowledges that her life is no longer her own. Becoming his disciple requires counting the cost of discipleship, loving Jesus supremely above all other relationships, and counting nothing as one's own (Luke 14.26, 33). Not only that, it also demands that we love one another just as he loved us (John 13.34). The character of the community of disciples is the key to mission and discipleship formation in a world of sin, brokenness, pain and egotism. Disciples are those who continually hear and obey the words of the master (John 8.31). To hear is to obey, and hearing the Word is the only way to the faith.

All of the above must be taught with specific applications worked out in each culture and with each new generation. Discipleship is not just memorizing principles; it is a total devotion to Christ and one another for a lifetime. Discipleship must be lived out in the community with God at the centre. One God, one faith and one mission are at the heart of discipleship. Furthermore, all Christians are called to be witnesses unto Christ in the power of the Holy Spirit. There are also many imperatives addressed to disciples. For instance, the Scriptures demand that the disciples of Christ be holy and perfect in love (1 Peter 1.15).

The early Pentecostals wanted to warn the Church that Christ was coming back for a bride without spot or wrinkle, undefiled and going about the Father's business. The warning to the

Church and the witness to the nations were and are urgent. His coming is imminent but indeterminate; he is coming soon, but no exact date is known except by God. This alerts Christians to live in godly reverence (i.e. fear of the Lord) and love. If we love him, we keep his commandments and shun evil; this should not, however, lead to legalism or libertinism. Also, as his disciples, we are to take seriously our social obligations. For this reason, it is significant to note that 'Church of God Practical Commitments' states: 'It should be our objective to fulfil our obligations to society by being good citizens, by correcting social injustices, and by protecting the sanctity of life.'[19]

Pentecostals still remember the past legalism and harshness that passed for holiness; however, legalists are not nearly so prominent today as the libertines who fail to observe scriptural limits and injunctions and turn liberty into licence to sin. The witness of the Church is greatly hindered by Christians who are no different from the world except in their church attendance. Being a witness is obeying. It is the faith that works through love that truly justifies and becomes a way of life so that believers become the holiness and righteousness of God in this world. Christians cannot be the light of the world while walking in darkness (1 John 1.5–7), ignoring injustice and dire human need, and practising the works of the flesh (Galatians 5.13–21). Social action ministry from first to last should be the gospel in action. The testimony of Jesus is the spirit of prophecy. We should be aware of those whose partisan politics constitute a new self-justification and legalism.

The Church that would have a credible witness must have a holy worship which culminates in a godly witness in words and deeds. This will require the intentional cultivation of purity and the fruit of the Spirit (Galatians 5.22–25). The Church must be a holy family caring for her sons and daughters, especially when so many are growing up without a married mother, a father or a safe, caring home. The Church ought not ask its government to legislate what the Church has refused to practise. Compassionate care among and with the poor, who have faces and names, is the legitimate beginning of all private and public gospel witness.

But this also will mean teaching others the seriousness of sin. In Galatians 5.19–21, the works of the flesh are listed: adultery, fornication, uncleanness, lewdness, idolatry, sorcery, hatred, contentions, jealousies, outbursts of wrath, selfish ambitions, dissensions, heresies, envy, murders, drunkenness, revelries and the like. All the works of the flesh are social sins needing social and spiritual action and deliverance. We are told that those who practise these things, in or out of the Church, will not inherit the kingdom of God. By practising sin, they become what they practise. They choose another god, another community and another destination. Being separated from the world and unto Christ, we are to be temples of the Holy Spirit and God's royal priesthood. Those who are Christ's have crucified the flesh, its passions and desires. This is mortification, or the negative side of sanctification (see Galatians 5.24). Other representative Scriptures which explain these tests of fellowship in everyday language are Romans 1.18–32; Ephesians 4.17–32; 5.1–7; 1 Corinthians 6.9–20. These behaviours represent disobedience, rebellion and rejection of salvation in Christ. In Hebrews 10.26–29, we are warned that if we knowingly, willingly continue to sin, there is no more sacrifice to avail for us. In effect, we have trampled the Son of God underfoot and counted the blood of covenant, by which we were sanctified, a common thing; most urgently, we have insulted the Spirit of grace, apart from which there is no grace. The writer of Hebrews thus warns of fiery judgement and indignation against such rebels (Hebrews 10.26–31).

The Church that has the one holy God as her God, and confesses the one holy faith in that God, will forfeit her witness and mission by rebellious and presumptuous behaviour. No matter what so-called prophets of grace may say, we cannot turn the

Word into a lie and become a law unto ourselves, hinder others and walk in darkness, and then expect to inherit the kingdom of God. Church discipline requires instruction, correction, reproof, rebuke and restoration of the fallen. The Bible is not a mere collection of man-made rules. It is the Word of God.

The one people of God, comprised of people from every race, ethnicity, social class and nation, is to be an example of true unity and is equally open to all to participate according to the gifts and talents given to each. This gathering is where all are 'laity', the people of God. Participation in this fellowship requires leaders who lead under the influence of the Holy Spirit and serve the Church for Christ's sake, following his example.

Godly leadership is essential to the true 'church militant' which takes on and engages dark powers and oppressive spirits, and the leaders learn a true spiritual leadership by noting how the Spirit operates:

- the Spirit always bears witness to Christ and not self;
- the Spirit leads into all truth and not confusion;
- the Spirit forms godly character, fruit of the Spirit, in all the body;
- the Spirit seeks to fill all and to dispense gifts as needed;
- the Spirit seeks to assist the body through the discerning of spirits;
- the Spirit brings clarity, not confusion, through teaching and illumination;
- the Spirit convicts the world of sin, righteousness and judgement.

The Spirit-filled leader will therefore exemplify these tenets by

- striving to lift up Christ, and not self;
- leading the Church to test all things by Scripture;
- striving to present all believers perfect (whole, complete) in Christ;

- assisting the congregation in a discernment process involving the Spirit, Scripture and the faithful;
- proclaiming the whole counsel of Scripture under the anointing of the Spirit and seeking the unity of the Church in the midst of confusion, doubt, defection and spiritual opposition;
- seeking training and continuing to learn for a lifetime, as taught by the Holy Spirit and anointed teachers;
- ministering with humility, compassion and patience, longing for all to experience something of 'heaven below' with God in our midst;[20]
- leading in mission and vision for the congregation or denomination in light of the ultimate vision of the kingdom of God, when all will be 'holiness unto the Lord'.

A few decades ago, John McKay, looking over the whole world and opining as to what the future Church would look like, suggested that the two leading influences would be a reformed Catholicism and a mature Pentecostalism.[21] This mature Pentecostalism should be accountable to the Lord and his people, true to its original vision and full-gospel mission; it should pay much more attention to the discipleship of its ministers and members and seek to manifest true holiness of heart and life, both social and personal. The Church of Pentecost was a new political power in the world, with the power of the Spirit anointing persons from every race, gender, nation, class and other grouping. Pentecostalism today must re-vision, more deeply and reverently, and transmit the faith that will sustain us in the increasingly challenging days ahead, addressing both the spiritual and social issues facing contemporary churches.

Any church that has the triune God always at the centre of its faith, that embraces a living faith working through love and engages in a holy discipling formation, that lives as a family in a heartless world and fights the right enemy (and not one another), shares a bright, burning vision of God's future for the

Church and the universe. This could be our finest hour if we act out of God's abundance and not our scarcity. The shared longing for our Church in this regard is ably and beautifully expressed in a time-honoured hymn of the Church:

> The Church's one foundation, Is Jesus Christ her Lord,
> She is His new creation, By Spirit and the Word.
> From heaven He came and sought her, To be His holy
> bride;
> With His own blood He bought her, And for her life
> He died.

> Elect from ev'ry nation, Yet one o'er all the earth,
> Her charter of salvation, One Lord, one faith, one
> birth;
> One holy name she blesses, Partakes one holy food,
> And to one hope she presses, With ev'ry grace
> endued.

> 'Mid toil and tribulation, And tumult of her war,
> She waits the consummation, Of peace forevermore;
> Till, with the vision glorious, Her longing eyes are
> blest,
> And the great Church victorious, Shall be the Church
> at rest.

> Yet she on earth hath union, With God the Three in
> One,
> And mystic sweet communion, With those whose rest
> is won;
> O happy ones and holy! Lord, give us grace that we,

Like them, the meek and lowly, On high may dwell with Thee.[22]

---

# Notes

1 See D. W. Dayton, *The Theological Roots of Pentecostalism* (Grand Rapids, MI: Baker Academic, 1987), pp. 35–81.

2 M. Chaves, *American Religion: Contemporary trends* (Princeton, NJ: Princeton University Press, 2011), pp. 33–41. Observing the rise of the 'none' category in North America, Chaves notes: 'Importantly, the increase in being "spiritual but not religious" is happening because nonreligious people are more likely to say they are spiritual, not because people are less likely to say they are religious. In 1998, 24 percent of people who were slightly or not at all religious said they were at least moderately spiritual; that increased to 35 percent in 2008 . . . the less religious also are showing more interest in "spirituality"' (pp. 40–1).

3 W. Granberg-Michaelson, *From Times Square to Timbuktu: The post-Christian West meets the non-Western Church* (Grand Rapids, MI: Eerdmans, 2013), pp. 7–12.

4 See Dorotheos of Gaza, *Discourses of Dorotheos of Gaza* (Omaha, NE: Patristic Publishing, 2019).

5 S. J. Land, *Pentecostal Spirituality: A passion for the kingdom* (Cleveland, TN: CPT Press, 2010), pp. 3–48; see also S. J. Land, 'Pentecostal Spirituality: Living in the Spirit', in L. Dupre and D. E. Saliers (eds), *Christian Spirituality III: Post-Reformation and modern* (New York: Crossroad, 1990), pp. 479–99.

6 D. Wheelock, 'Spirit-Baptism in American Pentecostal Thought', PhD dissertation, Emory University, 1983, p. 210. See also E. L. Waldvogel, 'The "Overcoming Life": A study in the Reformed evangelical origins of Pentecostalism', PhD dissertation, Harvard University, 1977. For the Wesleyan origins of the Pentecostal movement, see also V. Synan, *The Holiness-Pentecostal Movement in the United States* (Grand Rapids, MI: Eerdmans, 1971).

7 See M. E. Dieter, *The Holiness Revival of the Nineteenth Century* (Metuchan, NJ: Scarecrow Press, 1980).

8 For a comparative analysis between Calvin and Wesley, see

D. A. D. Thorsen, *Bringing Belief in Line with Practice* (Nashville, TN: Abingdon Press, 2013).

9 We should observe that the natural state of creation is without sin. The 'natural' state referred to here has to do with what became natural in terms of our fallen (not 'created') being and existence. To speak accurately, then, sin is an aberration from the origin and destiny of human beings insofar as God created us as good and intends to redeem us from our fallen state for the life that is to come.

10 Although sin has affected all dimensions of our being and existence in our fallen state, God has not withdrawn the possibility of God's redeeming grace. Wesley spoke of this particularly in terms of God's 'prevenient grace'; see Randy Maddox, *Responsible Grace: John Wesley's practical theology* (Nashville, TN: Kingswood Books, 1994), pp. 83–90.

11 J. Calvin, *Institutes of the Christian Religion*, ed. J. T. McNeill, trans. F. L. Battles, vol. 2 (Philadelphia, PA: The Westminster Press; London: SCM Press, 1960), Book III, Chapter 21, Paragraph 13.

12 J. Wesley, *The Works of John Wesley*, 3rd edn, vol. 10 (Nashville, TN: Baker Books), p. 266.

13 Calvin, *Institutes of the Christian Religion*, Book III, Chapter 24, Paragraph 12.

14 Wesley, *Works*, vol. 10, p. 229.

15 Wesley, *Works*, vol. 10, pp. 366–7.

16 H. B. McGonigle, *Suffering Saving Grace: Studies in evangelical history and thought* (Waynesboro, GA: Paternoster, 2001), p. 310.

17 See D. Moody, *The Word of Truth: A summary of Christian doctrine based on biblical revelation* (Grand Rapids, MI: Eerdmans, 1981).

18 Land, 'Pentecostal Spirituality', pp. 6–7.

19 'Church of God Practical Commitments: Social obligation', <http://www.churchofgod.org/practical-commitments/social-obligation>, accessed 6 January 2020.

20 See H. H. Knight III, *Anticipating Heaven Below: Optimism of grace from Wesley to the Pentecostals* (Eugene, OR: Cascade Books, 2014), esp. pp. 229–48. John Wesley held that the believer's vision of heaven is correlated with how she or he lives out salvation on earth: 'Whoever will reign with Christ in heaven must have Christ reigning with him on earth' (p. 229).

21 See Cheryl Bridges Johns, 'The Adolescence of Pentecostalism: In search of a legitimate sectarian identity', in *Journal of the Society for Pentecostal Studies*, 17.1 (1995), p. 3.
22 S. J. Stone, *Hymns of the Spirit* (Cleveland, TN: Pathway Press, 1969), p. 116.

# 4

# Pentecostalism and the Prosperity Gospel

## JOEL EDWARDS

## Heritage and heroes

When I registered as a theological student at London Bible College in 1972, I walked into a culture shock which is still continuing. What was, up to that point, a sheltered subculture of black classical Pentecostalism, opened out into a much wider evangelical world which occasionally seemed apostate.

It was, in fact, a process of re-education. Theological giants, who were known and revered across the evangelical world, were strangers to me. Conversely, some of my most influential heroes, such as A. A. Allen, Morris Cerullo and T. L. Osborne, often came up for condemnation. Since that time, my pilgrimage has been about covering wider ground without losing my Pentecostal orientation.[1]

This journey took me to the heart of British evangelicalism in 1988, where I served for more than 20 years. As director of the Evangelical Alliance UK (EAUK), one of my most troubled moments was presiding over the expulsion of Morris Cerullo World Evangelization Ministries in 1996. The trauma led to a theological consultation on the Prosperity Gospel and subsequently to the publication of *Faith, Health and Prosperity*, edited by Andrew Perriman, in 2003.[2]

# Christian compliance and contradictions

The starting point is to recognize that 'much of the Movement is evangelical'.[3] As Perriman suggests, its success may be due in part to the extent to which it has 'embraced certain core elements of Christian truth . . . that evangelicals have simply not taken seriously enough.[4] In fact, the basis of faith of the Universal Church of the Kingdom of God UK would not exclude it from membership of EAUK.[5]

But, in very basic terms, prosperity theology sits on the edge of Christian orthodoxy for important reasons. First, for its over-emphasis on financial and material gain as the authentication of faith. Second, for the wider concerns about fideism this has led to – effectively making faith an efficacious supplement or substitute for the cross.

The modern Word of Faith movement has been attributed to the pioneering work of Kenneth Hagin, followed by Kenneth and Gloria Copeland. But the movement has also been associated with faith brand-names such as Morris Cerullo, Creflo Dollar, Eddie Long, David Yongi Cho, Ray McCauley, Fred Price, T. D. Jakes and a host of others: Matthew Ashimolowo, Benson Idahosa, Pastor Enoch Adeboya. And it needs to be said that this list could be extended significantly if the names of others in Latin America and Africa were to be added.

But deeper theological concerns have been associated with the earlier influences of Christian Science and the New Thought movement of people like W. W. Kenyon. The problems raised by these influences include concerns about the supremacy of faith, the 'spiritual death' of Jesus, the power of visualization and over-identification with the divinity of Christ.

Having said all that, it is important to stress that there is no one monolithic Prosperity Gospel. It is also necessary, however, to point out significant similarities between prosperity teachers.

They all draw very deeply on a reliance on the Bible; they are committed to theological positivism; preaching and media are central to their craft. They invariably emerge from poverty or personal sickness, having encountered some powerful personal intervention. And they all have a Pentecostal pedigree. As Perriman reminds us, the movement 'overlaps to a considerable extent with mainstream Pentecostalism'.[6]

But it also shares historic roots with ministries such as that of George Müller, Keswick[7] and the Holiness/faith-cure/Pentecostal ideals.[8] And as Paul Freston argues, similarities may even be traced back to the Patristic period.[9] Prosperity theology did not emerge in a social vacuum and should therefore be located in its *socio-religious* context. It is clear that the faith movement and its subsequent prosperity message was in part a reaction to the spiritual lethargy of the late nineteenth-century church, destabilized by secular rationalism and losing ground to the New Thought movement.[10] With its roots in Pentecostalism, the faith movement, commercialized to become a gospel of wealth, set itself the task of transitioning from the *via negativa* of faith to a *via positiva* faith[11] rooted in a re-reading of the New Testament and a God who acts in the material world.

This study therefore takes place against the realization that Pentecostalism's global tendency towards prosperity cannot be understated in the twenty-first century. As David Muir reminds us:

> With estimated annual growth of Pentecostal-Charismatic churches at the rate of 20 million, and with a worldwide membership of over 543 million, it is, perhaps, easy to understand [David Martin's] claims of the global shift in the 'religious market place' which is characteristically Pentecostal.[12]

Prosperity and Pentecostalism is in effect a barometer of how the growing Christian community is exploring an important theology of empowerment. Evidently, prosperity theologies have emerged from a compound of cultic, evangelical, Pentecostal and socio-economic factors. It is as though a neo-Pentecostalism is providing a holistic theological dialectic or counter-argument to a Christian faith that hasn't worked for many poor Christians who are looking for answers to economic and physical oppression. Paul Freston suggests that, as a 'revolt against fatalism', prosperity theology rejects a European approach to suffering.[13] And these ideas are working both with and against the grain of *existing* theological ideas.

Freston draws attention to a 2006 survey of ten countries demonstrating that in all cases a very large percentage of the religious population *already* believed in some degree of prosperity. When asked, 'Does God grant prosperity to believers?' 64 per cent of non-Pentecostal religious people in Brazil agreed. The Pentecostal response took this to 83 per cent.[14] This shows that although Pentecostals in certain social settings believe in prosperity, in many instances they are reflecting and often amplifying belief systems that already exist.

With this in mind, perhaps McConnell is right to pronounce the Prosperity Gospel as 'material' rather than 'formal heresy'[15] which is going through a productive and yet hazardous theological adolescence typified by ethical tantrums. In this stage, it remains committed to an evangelical distinctive while wrestling to deal with the dichotomy between spirit and matter, faith and finance. The horror is that it seeks to do so with a myopic ecclesiology and without a serious historical perspective.

# Holiness ethics and prosperity

As a movement that has emerged from the Holiness/Pentecostal traditions of the late nineteenth and early twentieth centuries, prosperity theologies have attempted to link righteousness and prosperity.[16]

In his study of Apostle Guti's Zimbabwe Assemblies of God, Africa (ZAOGA), David Maxwell has demonstrated this dichotomy precisely – particularly with regard to the movement in Africa and Latin America. Once saved, the individual is brought into a pietistic community where a double makeover takes place: first to renew 'inner purity' and then to serve the church's needs within and beyond the congregation. This entails Bible study, prayer and discipline. Believers are called to a higher ethical code, avoiding addiction, infidelity and debt, so that the 'new Pentecostal male becomes less predatory, more able to care for the children of his marriage'.[17] In this regard, even anecdotal evidence suggests that the broad stream of prosperity communities have very active family enrichment ministries in which couples are encouraged to build positive families.[18] In the African context, Maxwell also draws attention to the rejection of negative ancestral practices, cultic behaviour and witchcraft.[19] Prosperity offers security[20] by diverting its adherents away from poverty and 'slipping over the edge'.[21] For example, Pastor Enoch Adeboya, general overseer of the Redeemed Christian Church of God, presides over churches in more than 170 nations and promotes a clearly moderate prosperity message with all the accessories of the Prosperity Gospel. However, the concept of holiness and integrity sits at the very heart of his teaching.[22] During a formal interview he linked integrity and holiness to anti-corruption:

> If your number one goal is heaven, then your number one goal is holiness . . . The more we impress on the people the need for holiness, then they will begin to see that you cannot claim to be holy and corrupt at the same time.[23]

The prosperity movement has an important Achilles heel: a faith that measures its success in material wealth nurtures its own ethical failure. The 'right to wealth' ethos has created entrepreneurial environments with poor accountability, poor governance and short cuts in fundraising ethics. In many instances, organizations founded by devotees of the Prosperity Gospel have charitable, non-profit status while operating with a corporate ethos.

There is no suggestion that prosperity preachers are intrinsically less moral than any other section of the Christian community; but the real cause for concern has to do with the lack of accountability which makes them – and their followers – more vulnerable. And all this is of particular importance at a time when faith communities in general and the Christian community in particular have become a part of a growing culture of corruption. It's a sad indictment that the cost of 'ecclesiastical crime' mushroomed from an estimated US$300,000 in 1900 to US$32bn in 2010, with predictions that it will rise to US$60bn in 2025.[24] In addition, the triumphalism associated with prosperity theology tends to neutralize its rhetoric about 'sin', holiness and financial integrity.

In 2000, as a response to these weaknesses, Kenneth E. Hagin published *The Midas Touch: A biblical approach to balanced prosperity*.[25] The study, which aimed at 'avoiding abuse and false practices'[26] in prosperity theology, included Hagin's 'list of priorities for holding meetings' designed to encourage integrity in public gatherings.[27] To date, it is not yet clear just how influential this document has been.

# Idolatry and the superman syndrome

The Bible is clear in its condemnation of idolatry (see Exodus 34.17; Leviticus 26.1; Numbers 33.52; Acts 15.29; 17.16; 1 Thessalonians 1.9; Revelation 9.20). Overwhelmingly, this condemnation is levelled at the use of totemic symbols of Yahweh or 'false gods'. Simply put, idols diminish and desecrate God's sovereignty by displacing him in the human heart. Although the prosperity movement shares Reformation cautiousness about images and idols, it promotes a culture of high-profile, powerful charismatic leaders. The Word of God is respected, but it is usually mediated through larger-than-life personalities. As Coleman graphically describes it, 'the most significant objects are the lectern, from which the sermon is preached, and the television cameras.'[28]

This 'superman syndrome' that appears indispensable to prosperity theology has become a substitute for the liturgical priesthood, the charismatic teacher of revelation. Prosperity preachers tend to present themselves as unique vessels of insider information coming directly from God and providing new awareness and liberation for the listener. This inevitably elevates the preacher to a status and authority without which the Bible itself remains little more than interesting literature.

This needs-based teaching is a two-edged sword. On the one hand, it clearly has support in Scripture. Invariably, God supplies our needs (Isaiah 58.11; Matthew 6.11; Luke 11.3; Philippians 4.19) through other human agencies (1 Kings 17.1–16; Isaiah 58.10; Acts 27.3). Indeed, it is wrong to condemn the idea of 'felt need' as a distortion of the gospel.[29] Quite clearly, Jesus responded to the felt needs of many who came to him, and for whom his miracles of healing would have had significant socio-economic and societal implications (Matthew 9.27; Mark 10.46–51; Luke 17.12).

We should applaud ministries meeting 'felt needs'; but idolatry begins when personality deflects from the Lordship of Christ or superimposes itself on the authority of the Bible. This happens in all religious communities, but the idolatry which ensues with some prosperity 'options' has everything to do with the merchandising of this status to such an extent that 'payment for service' leads to significant levels of wealth generated entirely from within the internal trading systems created and sustained by its leaders. And usually this practice is sustained by so-called 'laws' and 'principles' invented to maintain the aura of authority which is then traded on. In Coleman's view, this is fuelled by 'persuasive' and 'performative roles' in which 'an evangelical economy is constructed wherein the cultivation of faith involves the mass consumption of goods in the form of books, cassettes, and videos'.[30] It is what has been described as a 'technology of power'.[31] In this environment it is difficult to extricate the idolized personality of the preacher from the content of the material.

Even if one allows for an element of biblical 'revelation', the danger of a 'faith in faith' movement, in which this new magisterium of 'laws'[32] and 'principles' emerge, creates huge dangers for our understanding of how 'inspiration' truly works in relation to the canon of Scripture. Perriman summarizes this well:

> In constructing spiritual laws we take what is intrinsic to the character and mind of God and purpose of God and externalize it. We take such essential qualities as faithfulness and compassion and translate them into legal apparatus that may in principle be operated without dealing directly with God. In effect it produces a form of deism differing from classic deism only in that it incorporates the miraculous into the system; but the God of the system is pushed into the background.[33]

In grappling with the dichotomy between the material and spiritual world, prosperity preachers have unwittingly found themselves dancing between very old theological landmines. From views on Christ's spiritual death to our life in Christ, the theology has courted a series of 'material' heresies. This confusion has resulted in some defective views of the Trinity, as much as a confused doctrine of human nature. Both Copeland's famous exhortation that 'you are all God' and Cerullo's outburst, 'You're not looking at Morris Cerullo; you're looking at God. You're looking at Jesus!'[34] are worrying. This is not because these men set out to diminish the sovereignty of Jesus Christ; they simply have no reference to historical theology.

This emphasis on power avoids the ethical struggles of our now-not-yet life in the kingdom (Romans 7 and 8), and substitutes this tension for an unChristian triumphalism that fails to prepare believers for the inevitable moments of vulnerability. It leaves them ill-equipped to deal with weakness in other people. It's idolatry in that, inadvertently, it makes us self-appointed champions and we lose the thrill of God's power at work in our weakness (Romans 5.6; 2 Corinthians 12.8–9).

# A strategy for engagement

How we respond to this neo-Pentecostal movement is of paramount importance. Joe Aldred's impatient response draws a parallel to 'the sin of simony': 'What I am clear about is that I know of no account in Jesus' ministry linking money to miracles.'[35] Mark Sturge is willing to concede that the Prosperity Gospel raises fundamental questions about God and wealth; and given its 'redemption and lift' effect, 'it has a significant sociological and psychological part to play in the life of the church.'[36] In his more detailed paper on the socio-political impact of prosperity and Pentecostalism, David Muir suggests, 'The growing influence of what is known as the "prosperity gospel" has implications for both the formation of capitalist attitudes and activities, and for shaping political activism.'[37]

Something of that reality is reflected in Richard Burgess's study of the Redeemed Church of God movement. Burgess's observation is that educated and professional African Pentecostals are drawn to 'success orientated' theologies. In a 2007 survey, 78 per cent of members of the Redeemed Church of God felt that their finances had improved and 67 per cent said their job prospects were better as a result of the movement's message.[38]

Given the rapid growth of the faith and prosperity movement and its growing impact across poor and wealthier Christian communities alike, there is an urgent need for conversation. I know of very few settings in which there has been a genuine or sustained effort to reach out across the divide. I suspect that this is a theological as much as a cultural stalemate. Many prosperity communities are thriving and hold up biblical evidence to suggest they are right. They operate successful ministries and limit their conversations to avoid theological debates that throw them off course.

In any event, most prosperity leaders emerged from very humble backgrounds and have risen to enjoy power and status far in excess of their more intellectual Christian cousins. Indeed, their personal success and prosperity embody the very 'rags to riches' truth of the message they preach. They themselves have become the truth of the prosperity they preach.

Most 'traditional evangelical/Pentecostals' who belong to affluent churches have less need of a God who acts to heal or provide a house and car. The Prosperity Gospel and its audacious faith have little cultural or theological attraction for these Christians.

There is much to be very cautious and concerned about, but addressing the issue as 'Christianity in crisis'[39] is unlikely to open up the doors to progress and better understanding across the cultural and theological divides.

So here I want to suggest some rules of engagement in our response to the Prosperity Gospel.

First, if there is to be better understanding, it will have to begin with the much older Christian traditions, which should be more at home with the 'long game'. Traditional Pentecostalism should also be willing to learn from a closer conversation. And we should do this by recognizing prosperity theology as a younger family member rather than a total outcast.

It seems to me that prosperity preachers have much more in common with the New Testament than with the New Age movement. And even where they have drawn from New Thought philosophies, it is possible that this was done in order to copy the *language* rather than the *conviction* of New Thought ideas in the same way that the New Testament colonized Greek philosophy in the first century.[40]

Given the frequency with which scholars have linked Max Weber's Protestant ethic with the development of prosperity theology, one wonders if the movement is comprised of Reformation instincts. Indeed, I would go as far as to say that the adherents of prosperity theology may be regarded as children of the Reformation rather than outright heretics.

Second, given its Holiness/Pentecostal heritage, modern Pentecostalism has more in common with prosperity than we care to admit – in terms of its ethics as much as its paradigms of power and the lived existential life of Christ. We would do better to recognize our likeness and difference as an important starting point in this debate.

And here I am fascinated by the differences between African and Caribbean Pentecostalism. Richard Burgess's observation about the professionalism of African congregations is a crucial explanation of the drift towards prosperity theology. In his study, Burgess cites Hunt's study of the Redeemed Christian Church of God. In Hunt's view, the movement is succeeding because it has abandoned traditional 'sectarian millenarianism' to embrace the values of materialism, career development and human fulfilment.[41]

This is in stark contrast to the strong second-coming teachings of Caribbean Pentecostalists, such as the New Testament Church of God, the Church of God in Christ and the New Testament Assembly. Let me suggest four reasons that make Caribbean Pentecostalism immune to prosperity:

1 Caribbeans have an inbred holiness 'culture' which behaves like a sleeping policeman against prosperity. Arlington Trotman helpfully identified holiness as the distinctive feature of black faith.[42] And this kind of withdrawing holiness, which Davidson Hunter describes as an Anabaptist 'purity from the world',[43] has the same effect.

2 The pre-millennial 'culture' is like an immunization jab against excessive materialism. Caribbeans are escapists in a way that Africans are not and this is expressed most powerfully in our 'songs of emancipation'. For example, at the end of a graduation with students who were mainly under 40, the closing song was 'Goodbye world, I'll stay no longer with you'. Such songs of emancipation or anticipation were particularly powerful during a recent funeral service in the Willesden New Testament Church of God:

- 'We shall arise, meet in the skies'
- 'Have you heard of the city in the skies?'
- 'He'll understand and say well done'
- 'Goodbye world, I'll stay no longer with you'
- 'No tears in heaven'

3 Less likely to have middle-class inclinations, Caribbeans are driven by material modesty and do not speak in terms of being 'head' or 'tail'. Caribbeans believe, not in opulence or poverty, but in 'functional wealth'. By comparison, African Pentecostals are much more at ease with chiefdoms, and Latin Americans are comfortable with ideas of political power.

4 British Pentecostals are probably more comfortable with the culture of social security: we are neither driven by the do-it-yourself materialism of the USA nor the struggle against abject poverty of African or Latin American settings.

My third observation is that it's very hard to write off the Prosperity Gospel purely as a cult. Its leaders' high-profile love of media and public ostentation is the very opposite of cult behaviour. Prosperity preachers are easily locatable!

And fourth, a discussion which begins with the recognition that prosperity has been a positive attempt to make up the deficit of a barren church harassed by secularism and losing confidence in a God who works in the material world is probably a better place from which to start the dialogue. A positive response to prosperity is not a licence for heresy. But it may remind us that God is probably less panicked by theological error than we often are.

With this in mind, let me revert to Perriman's words as a sound argument for further collaboration. The biblical argument is overstated, the eschatology over-realized, the idealism over-blown. But this is the rhetoric of motivation – what we would call exhortation. It aims to engender among ordinary believers, often in the context of intense worship, an excitement and confidence in the powerful reality of God. It drives us too far up the mountain of faith, to the point where the air becomes too thin and most of us struggle to breathe; but as, inevitably, we slip and tumble back down, we may yet find ourselves coming to rest nearer the summit up than we were before.[44]

## Notes

1 J. Edwards, *Lord Make Us One But Not All the Same: Seeking unity in diversity* (London: Hodder & Stoughton, 1999).
2 A. Perriman (ed.), *Faith, Health and Prosperity: A report on 'Word of Faith' and 'Positive Confession' theologies* (Carlisle: Paternoster Press, 2003), p. x.
3 D. R. McConnell, *A Different Gospel: A historical and biblical analysis of the modern faith movement* (Peabody, MA: Hendrickson, 1988), p. 19.
4 Perriman, *Faith, Health and Prosperity*, p. 17.
5 See <http://www.uckg.org.au/about-us.aspx>.
6 Perriman, *Faith, Health and Prosperity*, p. 17.
7 Perriman, *Faith, Health and Prosperity*, p. 60.
8 Perriman, *Faith, Health and Prosperity*, p. 76.
9 P. Freston, *Prosperity Theology: A (largely) sociological assessment* (Lausanne Movement, 2015), p. 7.
10 McConnell, *A Different Gospel*, pp. 47–8.
11 Perriman, *Faith, Health and Prosperity*, pp. 226–7.
12 Dr D. Muir, 'The Seductive Gospel: Liberation, politics and the pursuit of riches', presentation, Ghana University, July 2013. See

also David Martin, *Pentecostalism: The world their parish* (Oxford: Blackwell Publishing, 2002).

13  Freston, *Prosperity Theology*, p. 2.

14  Freston, *Prosperity Theology*, p. 5.

15  McConnell, *A Different Gospel*, p. 20.

16  Perriman, *Faith, Health and Prosperity*, p. 57.

17  D. Maxwell, 'Delivered from the Spirit of Poverty? Pentecostalism, Prosperity and Modernity in Zimbabwe', *Journal of Religion in Africa* 28.3 (1998), p. 353.

18  See <http://www.uckg.org.au/about-us.aspx>.

19  Maxwell, 'Delivered from the Spirit of Poverty?', p. 354.

20  Maxwell, 'Delivered from the Spirit of Poverty?', p. 366.

21  Maxwell, 'Delivered from the Spirit of Poverty?', p. 370.

22  Adeboya's most used text is Hebrews 12.14.

23  Interview, The Jesus Agenda, Part 2, programme 3, June 2011.

24  T. M. Johnson, D. B. Barrett and P. F. Crossing, 'Status of Global Mission, 2010, in the Context of 20th and 21st Centuries', *International Bulletin of Missionary Research* 34.1 (January 2010), p. 34.

25  K. E. Hagin, *The Midas Touch: A biblical approach to balanced prosperity* (Tulsa, OK: Faith Library Publications, 2000).

26  Hagin, *The Midas Touch*, p. 115.

27  Hagin, *The Midas Touch*, p. 122.

28  S. Coleman, 'All-Consuming Faith: Language, material culture and world transformation among Protestant Evangelicals', *Etnofoor* 9.1 (1996), p. 35.

29  M. S. Horton (ed.). *Power Religion: The selling out of the Evangelical church?* (Chicago, IL: Moody Press, 1992), p. 331.

30  Coleman, 'All-Consuming Faith', p. 29.

31  Horton (ed.), *Power Religion*, p. 327.

32  Of course Paul, more than any other New Testament writer, struggled with these 'laws' in constructing his Christian ethics and a New Testament Christian anthropology. However, the Prosperity Gospel has appropriated these principles to construct new frameworks of reproductive laws in the cosmos which take on a salvific life of their own.

33  Perriman, *Faith, Health and Prosperity*, p. 138.

34  M. Cerullo, *The End Time Manifestation of the Son of God*, Morris Cerullo World Evangelism Tape 1.

35 Dr J. Aldred, *Thinking Outside the Box: On race, faith and life* (Hertford: Hansib, 2013), p. 180.

36 M. Sturge, *Look What the Lord Has Done: An exploration of Black Christian faith in Britain* (Bletchley: Scripture Union, 2005), p. 141.

37 Muir, 'The Seductive Gospel', p. 18.

38 R. Burgess, 'African Pentecostal Growth: The Redeemed Christian Church of God', in D. Mayhew (ed.), *Church Growth in Britain, 1980 to the Present* (Farnham: Ashgate, 2012), p. 133. The figures come from a 2007 Commission on Integration and Cohesion, which showed that Pentecostalism provided significant economic integration.

39 H. Hanegraaff, *Christianity in Crisis* (Eugene, OR: Harvest House, 1993).

40 For example, it is perfectly possible that Kenyon's motivation in studying New Thought was both polemic and evangelistic; see McConnell, *A Different Gospel*, pp. 47–8. I find it intriguing that by McConnell's own evidence, at his death at the age of 80, Kenyon's magazine had a circulation of 20,000 and he had written 12 books, but at no point did McConnell provide any direct or primary source to convict him of being brainwashed by New Thought.

41 S. Hunt, 'Neither Here nor There: The construction of identities and boundary maintenance of West African Pentecostals', *Sociology* 36.1 (2002), p. 165, quoted in Burgess, 'African Pentecostal Growth', p. 133.

42 A. Trotman, 'Black, Black Led or What?', in J. Edwards (ed.), *Let's Praise Him Again: An African Caribbean perspective on worship* (Eastbourne: Kingsway, 1992), pp. 21–33.

43 J. D. Hunter, *To Change the World: The irony, tragedy, and possibility of Christianity in the late modern world* (Oxford: Oxford University Press, 2010), pp. 218–19.

44 Perriman, *Faith, Health and Prosperity*, p. 136.

# 5

# A Pentecostal appraisal of Scripture, reason, tradition and experience

## CHARLOTTE V. V. JOHNSON

## Introduction

I am a woman of the twenty-first century, born and raised in Britain and of West Indian heritage, Jamaican to be precise. I attend the Willesden New Testament Church of God. I became an active student of theology in 2014, having found myself increasingly interested and passionate about pastoral care. I am very much aware that I am standing on the shoulders of pioneers and others who paved the way so that I could become a member of the Pentecostal family, and engage in Christian mission and ministry from its perspective.

As a Pentecostal student of theology, I consider it a great privilege to be asked to contribute to this book, a follow-up to *Challenges of Black Pentecostal Leadership in the 21st Century*,[1] which also published lectures given to commemorate the life and work of Bishop Dr Oliver Lyseight. Here, I present a way of looking at the Wesleyan Quadrilateral from the perspective of Pentecostal theology and Pentecostal hermeneutic, in the interest of our growth and development within the Christian faith family.

# Wesley's methodological approach

The word 'hermeneutics' means the interpretation of biblical texts, wisdom literature and philosophical texts through the study of theory and methodology; in other words, it applies to the interpretation of Scripture. In 2 Timothy, Paul wrote to Timothy to instruct him to defend the truth, purity and standards of the message of Jesus in order to protect the Christian faith from any attempts at false teaching or negative impacts on the holy Scriptures. Furthermore, Paul declared that all Scriptures are given by the inspiration of God. This declaration underpins our Pentecostal position, our fervour to instruct and nurture members to know the holy Scriptures as the Word of God and develop the ability to defend its truth. Pentecostals believe in the inerrancy and the supreme authority of the Bible, which is therefore an essential source for spirituality and daily life. I have heard the Bible described as 'Basic Instruction Before Leaving Earth' and although I am not sure who came up with this expansion of the the acronym 'BIBLE', I think it captures both the essence and purpose of the Bible's content and the rationale for instructing believers to study and deepen their understanding of its content. Keith Warrington, in his book *Pentecostal Theology*, is affirmative in his statement that 'Pentecostals believe that the primary purpose of the Bible is to help them develop their experience and relationship with God, to be more available to the ministry of the Holy Spirit and a personal relationship with Jesus.'[2]

The interplay between Scripture, reason, tradition and experience offers an interesting methodological framework within which to scrutinize our Pentecostal theology and the challenges we face in our time. It was Albert C. Outler, a twentieth-century theologian, who gave this framework the name 'the Wesleyan Quadrilateral'.[3] The Quadrilateral was first developed during John Wesley's work as an Anglican minister in the eighteenth century, when he played a significant role in increasing the understanding of salvation and theology of God, especially for the laity. It was presented as a consistent methodological approach, based on Wesley's inductive and deductive reasoning coupled with his investigation of the evidence considered relevant to Anglican doctrine.

A great deal of work in developing theological ideas about the interconnection between Scripture, reason and tradition had already been carried out, over the centuries, by earlier Anglican theologians, with whom Wesley was familiar as an Oxford student and Anglican minister. Experience as a component was not, however, explicit in early Anglican perspective. It was Wesley who incorporated it into the method. He did so to acknowledge the significant role it played in relation to Scripture, reason and tradition and to present a more holistic understanding of religious beliefs to the ordinary man and woman of God.

# Scripture

When looking at Scripture as one of the sources or components of the Quadrilateral, it is important to emphasize that Scripture is regarded by Pentecostals as the primary source of religious authority in comparison to the other three. Scripture is seen as *prima scriptura*; that is, the first or above all other sources of revelation or communication between the triune God and humanity. Scripture is the sole infallible rule of faith and praxis. In Dietrich Bonhoeffer's words: '[The] Holy Scriptures do not consist of individual passages; it is a unit and is intended to be used as such. As a whole the Scriptures are God's revealing Word.'[4]

Wesley believed without a shadow of a doubt that the holy Scriptures encapsulated everything we need or require to believe in God, to love God and Jesus, as we live on this earth in preparation for eternal life while we await the second coming of the

Lord Jesus Christ. Wesley was known as 'the man of one book',[5] and the Bible was referred to as his second language. The phrase 'plain truth for plain people'[6] expressed his unwavering belief in and commitment to the role that Scripture plays in the life of committed Christians.

The authority and application of Scripture is fundamentally paramount to Pentecostals' perception of life and praxis, particularly through the message of salvation, grace and holiness. Access to salvation is via the Word. To illustrate the point, Wesley stated that 'faith and salvation – include the substance of the entire Bible, the marrow as it were, of the whole Scripture.'[7]

Drawing from Wesley, the following discipline might be instructive to us in interpreting Scripture and establishing a reference for our daily lives:

- Speak as the oracles of God; as found in 1 Peter 4.11. Apply the Scripture as a semantic mode to promote perfection and confirm God's words.
- Apply the literal sense to God's Word unless it leads to a contradiction of Scripture which makes a mockery or absurdity. The example commonly used to make the point is Romans 8.28 regarding predestination, which is contradictory to God's law.
- Avoid 'proof-texting' by interpreting the scriptural text without regard to its literary context.
- Use Scripture to interpret Scripture, in accordance with the analogy of faith and the application of parallel passages. Passages are parallel because they appear to deal with the same subject, although sometimes there are passages that are problematic because they appear to be contradictory and require God's ordained interpretation to understand the link to God's divine love.
- Commandments are God's law which are covered by promises given to people and society to operate, live and abide by morally in our Christian lives.

- Use God's wisdom to interpret Scripture appropriately, for example Romans 7.7–25 where Paul talks about spirituality in his aim to edify readers.
- Desire to apply the original text and the most appropriate translation to promote the Scriptures.

The sanctified life is an aspiration of Pentecostals, who are committed to the lifestyle that develops out of continuous examination, interpretation and application of Scripture.

# Reason

Although, according to the rationale behind the Quadrilateral, Scripture is considered to be the primary authority, it cannot operate on its own. Scripture depends on reason, which acts as a source for interpretation, and it is therefore an important and fundamental component of this methodological approach to theology. Wesley believed that reason and reasoning were unique gifts from God. Human reasoning is seen as an essential element alongside a person's moral and political capabilities. God, in his faithfulness and graciousness, allows reason to continue to function as an ability by which we communicate and understand, even though, due to sinful nature, humanity has fallen short of the grace of God. All thinking requires the involvement of reasoning as it is a part of the processing or channelling of thoughts and interpretation. Pentecostals are confident in the belief that the Holy Spirit facilitates the rational and cogent thinking of the believer to develop the spiritual sensitivity to discern and make choices for life and Christian witness that are in harmony with Scripture.

Wesley's sermon 'Original Sin' deals with the heart of human relationship and the knowledge of God through the application of Scripture.[8] As we apply the use of reason, we learn through the application of faith the invisible things of God – even his eternal power and Godhead – from the things that are made possible. It is by reading and accepting the truth of Scripture on the basis of our reasoned interpretation that we accept claims such as the one given by Jesus, 'All things are delivered unto me of my Father: and no man knoweth the Son, but the Father; neither knoweth any man the Father, save the Son, and he to whomsoever the Son will reveal him' (Matthew 11.27). In another of his sermons, 'The Scripture Way of Salvation',[9] Wesley preached about the importance of salvation and the role of faith as well as the capacity to discern the truth by reasoned interpretation, as cautioned in Colossians 2.8: 'Beware lest any man spoil you through philosophy or vain deceit, after the tradition of men, after the rudiments of the world, and not after Christ.'

This Scripture is an example of faith acting as an assurance by which reason is put into action through the application of wisdom and knowledge to encounter the gift of God, in this case, salvation. Therefore, the relevance of reason is less about justifying its importance as a distinctive component part of the Quadrilateral; rather, it is much more about the role reason plays in providing a logical facility which enables the application of Scripture to operate alongside tradition, and to some extent experience, guarding against the risk of limitless interpretation of the holy Scriptures and the nature of God.

Wesley was of the view that there is 'no method of bringing any to the knowledge of truth, except the method of reason and persuasion'.[10] The point being that reason is important, but not as important as the role and function of Scripture. Reason does not function independently, but plays a distinct and instrumental role in partnership with the other components of the Quadrilateral. Reason has been described as the 'candle of the Lord, given to us to help appropriate revelation within the context that the Bible is supreme above all other sources or documentation'.[11] The sentiment of the eleventh-century Christian philosopher St Anselm of Canterbury, 'Fides quaerens intellectum', meaning 'faith seeking understanding' or 'faith seeking intelligence',[12] adds clarity to this point.

Wesley clearly used reason to develop his theological thoughts and relied on reason in delivering the messages which led to Methodism. Pentecostals would recognize the role of this component of the Quadrilateral as a requisite for plausible interpretation of Scripture and its application to life, and would relate this process to the work of the Holy Spirit who reveals the wisdom of God to the believer. Reasoning, intellectualism or thinking skills – call it what you will – does not produce faith or salvation, but it serves as a vehicle for the Holy Spirit to make divine wisdom known to the believer. The Holy Spirit enables us to develop the faculty and capacity to think, understand and make sense of our faith. Hence the Pentecostal emphasis on embracing the mind of Christ and asking what Jesus would do in our response to the challenges and opportunities we encounter in life.

Reason as an aspect of the Quadrilateral approach to theological reflection has a role to play in the deliberations of Pentecostal ministers, scholars and theologians, and should be embraced as a tool to help us address some of the theological challenges we face in our homes, churches, communities and society at large, such as unnecessary traditions, social injustice and inequalities. As part of the Quadrilateral, reason is an invaluable tool and a credible method by which to engage in the development of Pentecostal hermeneutical and exegetical approaches to biblical texts.

# Tradition

Tradition as part of the Quadrilateral is intriguing as well as complex in terms of its correlation with history and historical factors in relation to church and religion. It provides an important point of reference and verification in relation to the other components of the Quadrilateral. While developing his methodology, Wesley called on the churches of the time to look to older institutions, rituals and praxis as a way of improving Christian standards of living and worship. In the desire for a more dedicated and sustainable Christian life, he drew on the traditions of the historical churches and in so doing introduced what became known as the 'programmatic approach' to the study of theology. Constitutional documents of the Elizabethan Reformation period, such as the Articles of Religion, the Homilies and the Book of Common Prayer, became important to Wesley in his yearning to clarify his understanding of his commitment to the theology in which he was indoctrinated and the revelation he believed he was experiencing. His scrutiny and findings of the value of the tradition of the Church of England led him to conclude that 'the Church of England is the most Scriptural national church in the world'.[13] He went on to draw from early religions and old doctrines, alongside the Anglican tradition, in order to develop and promote his theological thoughts on salvation, in the process giving birth to what has become known as Methodism.

Wesley's focus on the value of tradition in relation to the other three components, in the process of 'faith seeking understanding', inspired fresh thinking about both the apostolic faith and the liturgy enshrined in the tradition of the Church, and about their potential to enrich the Christian experience. He commended past Christian teachings, such as fellowship through feasts, gathering together to support one another, in what became known as the 'Methodists' distinctive teachings',[14] as a way of nurturing faith for spiritual growth in the 'way of salvation'.

With its use of the Quadrilateral approach to theological enquiry, it can be argued that, having its roots in Wesleyan Holiness, Pentecostalism's history in church tradition goes as far back as the Eastern Orthodox Church. Pentecostals are a part of a larger tradition than we might appreciate; as such, decisions about what we consider to be sacrosanct and what we disregard may well be one of the challenges we face in the twenty-first century.

As Pentecostalism progresses as an expression of the Christian faith, an established brand of Christianity, with its distinctive religious signifiers, it can also be seen to be making a contribution to the tradition of the Church and the tradition of religions. If 'tradition' is a valuable tool in helping us make sense of our faith, this raises some pertinent questions for us as Pentecostals. How much do we allow ourselves to learn from our tradition? How do we draw on the rich traditions of the faith of our fathers and mothers to inform our theology and hermeneutics? Ted Campbell, a theologian of Church history, offers an insightful statement on the merits of tradition as a tool in our quest for theological clarity:

> Our calling then, in recognising the authority of tradition in a Wesleyan sense, is not to favour an antiquated vision of the past; it is rather, the calling to value God's own work throughout the story of God's people, and to take courage and confidence in the faithfulness of God speaking to us in tradition beyond the witness of the biblical age.[15]

# Experience

'Experience' might be considered the Pentecostal barometer. However, with the use of the Wesleyan Quadrilateral, its role as a tool is best measured in relation to its complementary contribution to the other components. Experience formulates the critical foundation of human knowledge. The integration of knowledge and experience gives life to 'spiritually dead orthodoxy that demonstrated none of the living power and vitality of a personal relationship with God through Jesus'.[16] It is important to distinguish between empirical and experiential knowledge.

Empirical knowledge 'is founded on experience, observation, facts, sensation, practice, concrete situations and real events'.[17] It is otherwise known as 'a posteriori knowledge derived from sensory experience and is generally capable of public assessment'.[18] On the other hand, experiential knowledge tends to rely on understanding, insights or information derived from personal experiences. This type of knowledge depends on introspection or self-analysis, conscious states that tend to be private. It is in contrast to empirical knowledge but it is not the same as 'a priori knowledge', which is derived from reason without reference to experiential knowledge. As you may appreciate, personal experiences are difficult to assess publicly due to the fact that those experiences are individual and personal; therefore, others would have great difficulty in assessing an individual's experience without applying their own subjective judgement or views.

Pentecostals place a high value on their spiritual experiences. The Quadrilateral methodological theology provides a useful lens through which the 'Pentecostal experience' may be viewed, considered and decoded for the purposes of holistic spiritual formation and Christian witness in their various forms – for example preaching, teaching, mentoring, evangelizing and the production of learning resources. It would be interesting to see what impact and outcomes would become evident if Pentecostal leaders were to look through the Quadrilateral lens at the debatable five-fold ministry: apostles, prophets, evangelists, pastors and teachers, as found in Ephesians 4.11.

# The application of the Quadrilateral approach to the Pentecostal experience and practice of ministry

Since the early 1960s, we have seen the growth of many independent Pentecostal churches in Britain, particularly in large urban areas where there are significant black and minority ethnic populations. Unlike the historic churches, such as the Catholic, Anglican and other Protestant Christian faith groups, these Pentecostal churches, or assemblies as some are called, are often regarded as 'new' denominations without deep-rooted histories in Christianity and the global church.[19] Adherents may only perceive themselves as part of a given local church community, and as such may have no sense either of belonging to the wider Pentecostal movement or of its historical links with the wider Christian Church. As such, there is the danger that Pentecostals may become locked into a 'closed' space, a windowless room where genuine growth and expression of the Spirit-led life is stifled. The group may of course talk characteristically about the ability and freedom to worship God in a free and expressive manner; they may testify about salvation, sanctification, the experience of God's grace and their commitment to the command in Matthew 22.36–40: 'Love the Lord thy God with all thy heart, and with all thy soul and with all thy mind . . . and love thy neighbour as thyself.' But, beyond talk within the group, there is little evidence of connectivity with the wider Pentecostal story or, for that matter, the wider Christian Church. However, this is not an issue only for the black majority Pentecostal church. The question about how we as Christians can make time to engage more fully with Christian theology and allow ourselves to become more confident and effective in our private and public worlds would seem to be a growing challenge for many churches.

One of the most significant identifiers for Pentecostals – and in particular 'classical Pentecostals' – is 'speaking in tongues' as referred to in Acts 2.4–6. The normative model for Pentecostals is drawn from Acts 10.44–48. It would seem, however, that for many of us the experience of infilling or baptism in the Spirit is as much as we aspire to or are taught. The application of the Quadrilateral approach to our experience and practice of ministry might help us to become more effective in our personal and communal lives as Pentecostals.

Another feature of Pentecostalism is how worship is expressed. Worship is experiential. Pentecostals enter worship services in anticipation of 'how the Spirit leads'. While a service might be carefully planned, the leaders and congregation will not be perturbed if they 'feel' that the Spirit is leading in a different direction, even over a longer duration than planned. Jean-Jacques Suurmond describes Pentecostal worship services as 'the Word and Spirit at play . . . [in which everyone has a contribution to make] . . . with spontaneity and order [as] in a "jazz performance".'[20]

Wolfgang Vondey provides an insightful reflection on Suurmond's thoughts: 'this imagination is best described not as a story or performance of a drama but as a play.'[21] A play consists of a number of components such as storytelling, drama and scenes. The Word of God and the Holy Spirit play a distinctive role in Pentecostalism. Suurmond, along with others, is of the view that God provides, through Scripture, the essentials and configuration of the play, while the Spirit supplies energy and options. Therefore theological reflection, in the broader context, is mediated as a drama only insofar as it is the enduring yet unfinished dynamic that is orientated towards an encounter with God through the Holy Spirit.

The presence of God in the drama of Pentecostal worship will be acknowledged. There will be an air of expectation, a spiritual visitation through the demonstration of the 'gifts of the Spirit', with collective or congregational worship and prayer. Spontaneity and participation may to some extent be limited, with opportunities for the operation of the gifts of the spirit, liturgical dancing and expressive singing to take place in preparation for the preaching of the Word of God and the altar call, which usually comes at the end of the message. As Steven Studebaker has said,

[T]he Pentecostal movement is about being caught up in an experience of God's Spirit that transforms lives and empowers them to serve God in this theology. Not a theology that fractures the Christian communities, but a theological 'tongue' of the Spirit of Pentecost that contributes to the richness of the Christian community.[22]

Heightened pastoral care and spiritual sensitivity grounded in theological clarity is clearly needed in these services if everyone is to leave feeling blessed to be a blessing in their particular locale.

It would appear that in the mindset of some leaders, and subsequently of their congregations, there is a subtle yet definite shift towards placing the emphasis on a more communal encounter with God rather than an individual encounter. Emphasis is inadvertently put on the expectation of meeting with God corporately over and above meeting with God personally or intimately. So the testimonies, altar calls, tarrying for baptism in the Spirit and healing services, which are characteristic of the Pentecostal church experience, are no longer evident in many local churches.

It is useful to recognize that each particular Pentecostal church community will have its own definitive culture based on local factors including the specific history of the given church. The position and reputation of a church within a local community will be influenced by the ability to recognize and adjust to its changing landscape, thereby contributing to the future and history of the church. For example, the UK riots in 2011 may have revealed those churches with the ability to be sufficiently flexible and pragmatic to evangelize in that context, motivated by the belief that Christians are the salt of the earth and the light of the world while awaiting the imminent return of Jesus.

Reliance on Scripture as the primary authority is still a distinctive feature of Pentecostalism. It would however be a good thing if more, if not all, leaders in the movement made it their duty to seize every opportunity to utilize the Quadrilateral in whatever shape or form to facilitate the growth of biblically literate, wise, rooted and Spirit-filled believers and church communities.

There is a general view that Pentecostals are 'doers rather than thinkers'. However, thinking is a requisite for doing things well. Another throwaway comment is that Pentecostals are far more concerned and focused on soteriology (personal salvation) than ecclesiology or hermeneutics. We need to know who we are and what we have to contribute to the corporate witness of our faith, and do so with the courage, wisdom and spiritual sensitivity that comes with Spirit-baptism.

The leadership styles in many Pentecostal churches seem to be going through a period of transition. Various models are emerging to accommodate the varying groups and perceived needs of people at the local, regional and national, even global, level. Some Pentecostal denominations are centralized, operating from a headquarters. Some are decentralized and function independently, emphasizing their autonomy and freedom from perceived institutional distractions, such as hierarchical relationships and expectations. These independent churches will usually share fellowship with other like-minded churches from time to time. Many leaders are self-styled. Some have been mentored for their positions, some have had formal theological training and some have had a little of both. Suitably trained leadership at all levels within Pentecostalism is essential if the spiritual growth and development of each member is to be sustained alongside the 'sense of calling' to assume leadership roles and appointments within and beyond the local church.

A continuing challenge for Pentecostals, not unlike other Christian denominations, is how to make the message of Scripture appealing to the 'NOW' generation (young adults, aged 21–40) and engage them in training for current leadership roles, as well as in training future leaders.

The Wesleyan Quadrilateral provides Pentecostalism with an inclusive, expansive, solid and substantive paradigm for theological edification in an ecumenical setting. There would seem to have been a positive move in recent times for Pentecostals across the spectrum to engage in ecclesiastical dialogue and debate with others outside their own theological perspective. For example, the New Testament Church of God is a member of Churches Together in England, which hosts a range of ecumenical gatherings and facilitates church-led debates and activities with others in the wider society on societal issues and concerns. The Oliver Lyseight lectures provide opportunities for New Testament Church of God members to discuss theological matters in the company of those from other denominations. Along with Pentecostal theologians, biblical scholars, pastors and students in Europe, their counterparts in the New Testament Church of God have joined the European Pentecostal Theological Association (EPTA), allowing them to benefit from its forums, meetings and discussions, and from the research opportunities it facilitates for active fellowship, networking and mutual learning.

Tony Richie, in an article entitled 'Pentecostalism's Wesleyan Roots and Fruit', writes, 'I want to move beyond where I am without leaving behind where I have been.'[23] The principles of the Quadrilateral provide a fundamental platform on which current and future generations can continue to build in the interest of sustainable growth and development. The desire to shape and leave a legacy for future generations is becoming a driving force among denominations such as the New Testament Church of God. In addition, the Oliver Lyseight lectures, as well as the subsequent publications, are encouraging evidence of the determination to contribute to the Pentecostal heritage and legacy.

Winfield H. Bevins has said, 'If Wesley were here today he would take into account both the historical and contemporary events that have taken place in the last three hundred years especially in regard to the trajectory of the Pentecostal movement.'[24]

He is not here with us, but we can identify a growing number of Pentecostal theologians, scholars, church leaders and others around the world who are reflecting and offering insightful observations to inform the Pentecostal perspective and witness to our increasingly complex world. If we are to have any credibility in our witness and a plausible Pentecostal perspective to contribute to the social issues of our time, such as globalization, postmodernism, racial injustice and inequality, poverty and political corruption, to name a few, we need to probe our theology with an open mind and the willingness to use the appropriate language and communication skills to share the good and redeeming news of the kingdom.

Contextualization is becoming increasingly important when looking at one's faith from a theological perspective, and it has become imperative to adopt a holistic and comprehensive approach to addressing issues and taking agendas forward. This may include being mindful of dangers such as pluralism, which may lead to all religions being seen as equal when this is contrary to the Christian faith. It is clearly important to have an understanding of the sensitivities in the mix while being courageous enough to stand our ground in the situations in which we find ourselves. Miroslav Volf said that 'people of faith should consider practising hermeneutical hospitality'.[25] In order to search for truth and mutual understanding in the ecumenical context we should be prepared to listen attentively in order to gain some understanding of different perspectives and be well prepared to contribute our perspective. Such hospitality will not necessarily lead to agreement. However, a hospitable approach will promote harmonious relationships and good understanding of the various perspectives, as well as promoting respect for each other in a spirit of companionship rather than one of combat in the search and struggle for the wisdom and truth of our triune God.

Pentecostals believe that Scripture is the supreme authority of the Christian faith and therefore essential to their daily living as providing the source to spiritual living. Through the lens of 'experience', we can find a language that enables us to talk with confidence about life through the operation of the Holy Spirit. The holy Scriptures as God's authority set the standard for those who are called by God to live with the component parts of tradition. Scripture was and still is recognized as the primary component of the Quadrilateral, although it is insufficient on its own as a source for daily living. Reason acts as the channel for communication and rational thinking within the counsel and guidance of the Holy Spirit. The phrase 'faith seeking under-standing' positively reflects our continuing journey into new beginnings in our Christian pilgrimage. Our faith and hope in Christian discipleship encourage and inspire the desire to seek a deeper understanding of God's word, and, of course, this all leads to a more sophisticated development of hermeneutical practice and a more advanced Pentecostal spirituality. A dialectical presence in Pentecostalism allows reason, representing intellect, to take valued Pentecostal experience to another level through the application of the holy Scriptures as *prima scriptura*, guided by the Holy Spirit and backed up by the valid tradition of the Church. Pentecostals can therefore draw much from Wesley's Quadrilateral. To fully understand and grow in our faith, there is the need for a 'heads and hearts' engagement, a need to combine Scripture, reason, tradition and experience in our approach and methodologies for theological clarity.

# Conclusion

Understanding the interplay between Scripture, reason, trad-ition and experience provides a secure base in the quest to make sense of our faith. The quest for meaning will inevitably bring us to new beginnings. In this pursuit, we are faced with ques-tions of how comfortable we are to explore and consider new ideas and abandon false assumptions, and on what basis we would embrace new ideas and discard false assumptions. More importantly, how do we relate this to the 'saved' and the 'not yet saved' in our local communities, to the younger generation or the so-called millennials within or outside our congregations and Sunday schools? For example, how well equipped are we to address cyber-bullying, gangs defined by geographical post-codes, and so on?

As Pentecostalism continues to grow and position itself in the Christian community and the wider world, we will need to have clear understanding of our distinctiveness and identity; otherwise we could become a silent witness. If there is to be a future generation of Pentecostals, it is of vital importance that they are given the resources and skills to identify and articulate their historical and theological background with clarity and godly wisdom. Learning about and from past generations of Pentecostal leaders, which included people such as Charles Parham, Aimee Semple McPherson, William Seymour and Oliver Lyseight, is clearly a prudent endeavour in the interest of ensuring the future of Pentecostalism as a distinct member of the Christian family.

Wesley's Quadrilateral provides a tried and tested methodological approach and a credible resource to interrogate theology. It has the potential to advance theological reflection, to inspire teaching and learning about the fundamentals of the Christian faith, and provides a template to assist us in the pursuit of understanding and defending the distinctive characteristics of Pentecostal theology.

## Notes

1 P. Thompson (ed.), *Challenges of Black Pentecostal Leadership in the 21st Century* (London: SPCK, 2013).

2 K. Warrington, *Pentecostal Theology: A Theology of Encounter* (London: T&T Clark, 2008), p. 188.

3 A. C. Outler, 'The Wesleyan Quadrilateral – In John Wesley', Ameri-

can Theological Library Association Series 13, *Wesleyan Theological Journal* 20.1 (1985), p. 13.

4  D. Bonhoeffer, *Life Together* (London: SCM Press, 2015), p. 36.

5  Outler, 'The Wesleyan Quadrilateral', p. 13.

6  Outler, 'The Wesleyan Quadrilateral', p. 13.

7  Outler, 'The Wesleyan Quadrilateral', p. 13.

8  J. Wesley, 'Original Sin' (Sermon 44).

9  J. Wesley, 'The Scripture Way of Salvation' (Sermon 43).

10  D. A. D. Thorsen, *The Wesleyan Quadrilateral: Scripture, Tradition, Reason & Experience as a model of evangelical theology* (Grand Rapids, MI: Zondervan, 1990), p. 173.

11  E. Parker, 'Reason Is "The Candle of the Lord"', *The Calvinist International*, 8 September 2014, p. 1.

12  H. T. Kerr (ed.), *Readings in Christian Thought*, 2nd edn (Nashville, TN: Abingdon Press, 1990), pp. 82–3.

13  W. S. Gunter, S. J. Jones, T. A. Campbell, R. L. Miles and R. L. Maddox (eds), *Wesley and the Quadrilateral: Renewing the conversation* (Nashville, TN: Abingdon Press, 1997), p. 71.

14  W. H. Bevins, 'A Pentecostal Appropriation of the Wesleyan Quadrilateral', paper presented at the 34th annual meeting of the Society for Pentecostal Studies for the PNEUMA Foundation, 2005.

15  T. A. Campbell, 'Authority and the Wesleyan Quadrilateral', in C. Yrigoyen Jr (ed.), *The T&T Clark Companion to Methodism* (London: T&T Clark, 2014), pp. 61–72 (61–71).

16  Thorsen, *The Wesleyan Quadrilateral*, p. 129.

17  Thorsen, *The Wesleyan Quadrilateral*, p. 130.

18  Thorsen, *The Wesleyan Quadrilateral*, p 130.

19  A. H. Anderson, *Introduction to Pentecostalism* (Cambridge: Cambridge University Press, 2014), pp. 5–7.

20  J.-J. Suurmond, *Word and Spirit at Play: Toward a Charismatic Theology* (Grand Rapids, MI: Eerdmans, 1995), pp. 20–6.

21  W. Vondey, *Beyond Pentecostalism: The crisis of global Christianity and the renewal of the theological agenda* (Grand Rapids, MI: Eerdmans, 2010), p. 40.

22  Steven Studebaker, cited in C. E. W. Green, 'In Your Presence Is Fullness of Joy: Experiencing God as Trinity', in L. R. Martin (ed.), *Toward a Pentecostal Theology of Worship* (Cleveland, TN: CPT Press, 2016), p. 190.

23  T. Richie, 'Pentecostalism's Wesleyan Roots and Fruit', *Seedbed* (14 March 2014), p. 3.

24  Bevins, 'A Pentecostal Appropriation of the Wesleyan Quadrilateral, p. 1'.

25  M. Volf, 'A Voice of One's Own: Public faith in a pluralistic world', discussion draft for conference on The New Religious Pluralism and Democracy, 21–22 April 2005. Sponsored by Georgetown University's Initiative on Religion, Politics, and Peace, <http://irpp. georgetown.edu/conference.htm>

# Conclusion

## PHYLLIS THOMPSON

Two intrinsic merits of Pentecostalism are its global extent and the positively life-changing impact it has on the lives of its adherents. In identifying and discussing how we might best sustain and secure our virtues, the distinctiveness of Pentecostal theology is highlighted, while we note some challenges currently encountered alongside examples or signposts to opportunities for addressing them.

Theological clarity is a challenge in a world in which church and the Christian faith are no longer the norm, and the language available to talk about God is limited. For many in the western hemisphere, churches are associated with the elderly and have little appeal for young people. There is therefore a tendency for Church leaders to react by re-inventing themselves and their church services to provide what they consider to be the solution. Unfortunately, this often manifests itself as a theatrical performance with lights, sounds and 'celebrity'-style relationships between those in the pulpit and those in the pews, which, not surprisingly, alienates the mothers and fathers otherwise known as the 'pillars' of the church. Accommodating the range of generations we want in our churches is clearly not an easy task. Clarity about what is fundamental and what are considered to be the non-negotiables of Pentecostal theology is very important at all levels within the movement. Failure to achieve this will potentially lead to an ever wider gap not only between generations but also between the expressions of our belief and praxis. It is therefore of critical importance that opportunities are seized to enable theological clarity and confidence in the vision and ministry of the Pentecostal movement in all aspects of life, lest we embrace contrary ideas and belief systems merely to satisfy popular opinions of the day.

Direct focus on the strength of the Pentecostal brand of theology represented in this book is an important starting point in dealing with the challenges we face. What is it that Pentecostals have to offer to the universal Christian witness? With reference to Keith Warrington's consideration, one distinctive quality is the ability to appreciate and 'listen' to God through the ministry of the Holy Spirit. Theological clarity about the person and work of the Holy Spirit is fundamental. A personal experience of the Holy Spirit as a guide and partner in the life of the believer is of vital importance. With this understanding, individuals may not only seek to follow the leading of the Holy Spirit in their personal lives but also seek, in solidarity with members of their local church, to discern the will of the Holy Spirit in their times of worship, prayer and public witness, and to discern how best to address the challenges they encounter as Christians in their individual and corporate worlds. How well adherents are nurtured to appreciate and desire this virtue of Pentecostal belief and practice is a current concern for the movement.

Keith Warrington's piece is indicative of a challenge we have with gender-inclusive language when we seek to verbalize anything about the triune God. While 'God the Father' and 'God the Son' provide relational illustrations, it is problematic for some that God's feminine characteristics are not overt. The use of gender-appropriate language to communicate about the Holy Spirit presents further obstacles. How do we relate to the Spirit? And is the Spirit a 'he' or a 'she', or both? Many Pentecostals are conservative in their hermeneutics and exegeses, and the very thought of gender-neutral language is resisted for fear of succumbing to contemporary pressure. The effort of Pentecostal theologians is clearly a critical must to assist our clarity and discipleship endeavours.

# Conclusion

Adherents to the Pentecostal movement can be unwittingly trapped within a limited outlook on Pentecostalism. They may choose to walk away from their Pentecostal roots and the Christian faith if they think that what is on offer to them is irrelevant to their lives. How we communicate the fundamentals of our theology to the younger generation and the leaders of tomorrow – otherwise known as the millennials or Generation Y and the post-millennials or Generation Z – is in itself a major challenge. Where do we start? With doctrines and dogmas or with their everyday experience? Is there a shared language between seasoned Pentecostals and millennials with which to talk about God?

It is important to keep context in perspective if we want to develop a sustainable theology. If we do not do so, our theology and dogmas will be regarded as antiquated and unrelated to the realities of life, such as the experience of marginalized people and the impact of postmodernism on current ways of thinking and talking about God. It is Douglas Nelson's conviction that it would be in the interest of Pentecostals to recognize and address the contexts in which we live, and the potential of the knowledge and insights gained in the process, in order to enhance the development and articulation of our theology in relevant and credible ways. Drawing on the experience of black Americans to assist reflection on the experience of migrants in the British context and realities of the so-called 'black majority Pentecostal churches', we are urged as 'black' and 'white' Pentecostals to examine our pastoral sensitivity and missional focus. The connection between our hermeneutics and the hope of our faith is not always consistent or convincing. Revelation 7.9, for example, 'and, lo, a great multitude, which no man could number, of all nations, and kindreds, and people, and tongues, stood before the throne, and before the Lamb', presents a theological dilemma if some of the realities of current racial concerns are taken into serious consideration.

As for all traditions in the wider Christian Church, Pentecostal theology is brought under scrutiny by the proponents of post-modernism. Failure to develop a credible response to the questions posed from this viewpoint about our 'reading' of Scripture, our belief in Scripture as the inerrant Word of God, the issue of relative truth, and popular views about absolutes, will weaken our credibility. How we respond to the approach and perspectives of 'historical-critical' methods of biblical study is a challenge we must equip ourselves to address if our Pentecostal theology is to sustain its dynamism and revitalizing distinctiveness in the postmodern world.

Christian praxis with a Pentecostal nuance varies around the globe. Speaking from his North American experience, Steve Land shares his answers to some of the questions that motivate his theological quest. What are the characteristics of a Pentecostal and how can we disciple our membership? What daily disciplines should we, as Pentecostals, sanction for personal and social holiness? What benchmark do we use to change and develop our content and approach? What can we learn from other Christian communties to sharpen our Pentecostal perspective of the Christian faith? How do we decide what are the non-negotiables in the face of the challenges we encounter?

How these questions are addressed within the stream of Pentecostalism, and how answers are communicated and implemented, evidently varies from continent to continent. Steven Land is confident that a study of the history of Pentecostalism will reveal evidence of its roots in Wesleyan Holiness and, as such, will provide a sound basis for reflection and action.

Joel Edwards' story of his beginnings and his continuing journey in the Pentecostal movement illustrates a positive trajectory. However, it also draws attention to the inadvertently incomplete story of many who, unlike him, are left to meander in the rituals of the movement, with little or no opportunity for growth and meaningful engagement in the mission and ministry of Pentecostalism.

Another underlying challenge for Pentecostals in local, national and global contexts is that of succession. Gaps are becoming more and more evident as pioneers such as Oliver Lyseight pass on. There is clearly a need to inspire young men and women to embrace Pentecostal theology, and make appropriate preparations to assume spiritual and intellectual leadership roles in the missional focus of the church, to ensure that the Pentecostal fire remains alive.

The roles of routine Sunday schools and Bible study sessions within the movement in the formation of the Pentecostal believer are not to be overlooked, and neither is the role of the teachers to be underestimated. Valuing and resourcing teachers in local churches and the celebration of teaching and learning are vital means of a positive response to these challenges.

'Pentecost Sunday' could be an effective springboard for engaging those in the pew, pulpit and academy in critical reflection on our heritage, our heroes and heroines, and for celebrating the distinct contribution of Pentecostals to the mission of the wider Christian Church.

Reliable self-definition is a mark of growth and maturity. The attributes of a Pentecostal are best defined by ourselves rather than others. Arriving at a consensus at any level of a hierarchy can however be contentious. As the movement matures, be it in the local context or the national or global, hard questions must be asked and painful decisions will have to be made in order to achieve theological clarity and praxis. For example, there is a need for clarity about the negotiables and non-negotiables of Pentecostal theology and its distinctives, as well as a consensus on acceptable arbitrators and what the agreed processes and procedures should be for reconciling differences of opinion, particularly on major issues such as dogma within the Prosperity Gospel. Peer conversations offer effective starting points, with the potential for new beginnings, leading to unimagined paradigm shifts in what otherwise might become antagonistic relationships resulting in stalemate.

The Wesleyan Quadrilateral is offered by Charlotte Johnson as a valuable structured approach for reflection and action. She cautions, however, that in so doing, we should be careful not to overlook the richness embedded in the traditions of the wider Christian Church in which our history is deeply rooted. The merit of dialogue and engagement with ecumenical partners is presented as a positive and enabling opportunity to broaden the spectrum of options and outcomes. Rather than being protective, we are best advised to open ourselves to 'hearing' what the Spirit might be saying through the experience of the wider Christian Church family.

The propelling desire in addressing the challenges of Pentecostal theology in the twenty-first century is the wish to develop and sustain the legacy of Pentecostalism: the blessing of empowerment for living in the fullness of the Spirit-filled life. We hope and pray that this book will provoke and encourage further thinking about Pentecostalism, bring about greater clarity concerning our Pentecostal distinctiveness, strengthen the aspiration to live what we believe as Pentecostals, and enable us to defend the hope of our faith with confidence.

# Additional references

# Books and journals

Anderson, A. A., 'The Newer Pentecostal and Charismatic Churches: The shape of future Christianity in South Africa', *Pneuma* 24.2 (2002), pp. 167–84

Anderson, Allan Heaton, *An Introduction to Pentecostalism*, 2nd edn, Cambridge: Cambridge University Press, 2014

Aultman, Donald S. (ed.), *Faith of Our Mothers*, Cleveland, TN: Pathway Press, 2014

Aultman, Donald S. and Land, Steven J., *Faith of Our Fathers*, Cleveland, TN: Pathway Press, 2009

Jenkins, P., *The Next Christendom: The coming of global Christianity*, Oxford: Oxford University Press, 2002, p. 67

*Journal of the European Pentecostal Theological Association* 39.2 (September 2019)

Land, Steven J., *Pentecostal Spirituality: A passion for the kingdom*, Cleveland, TN: CPT Press, 2010

Liardon, Roberts, *God's Generals*, New Kensington, PA: Whitaker House, 1996

Maiden, John, 'Race, Black Majority Churches, and the Rise of Ecumenical Multiculturalism in the 1970s', *Twentieth Century British History* 30.4 (December 2019), pp. 531–56

Noel, Amber, 'Politics and Pentecostal Freedom', *Church of God Evangel* (July 2019), pp. 22–3

Oden, Thomas C., *How Africa Shaped the Christian Mind*, Downers Grove, IL: IVP, 2007

Volf, Miroslav, *A Public Faith: How followers of Christ should serve the common good*, Grand Rapids, MI: Brazos Press, 2011

Williams, Colin, *John Wesley's Theology Today: A study of the Wesleyan Tradition in the light of current theological dialogue*, Nashville, TN: Abingdon Press, 1960

Yung, H. 'Pentecostalism and the Asian Church', in Anderson, A. H., Tang, E. (eds), *Asian and Pentecostal: The Charismatic face of Christianity in Asia*, Oxford: Regnum, 2005, pp. 37–57

# Online

Kirk Franklin talks with Matt Crouch, Robert Morris and Dr Tony Evans on TBN's *Praise*, <https://www.youtube.com/watch?v=nm0PeMU7z2A&list=RDnm0PeMU7z2A&start_radio=1#t=38> or <https://youtu.be/nm0Pe-MU7z2A>, accessed 16 April 2020

# WE HAVE A VISION OF A WORLD IN WHICH EVERYONE IS TRANSFORMED BY CHRISTIAN KNOWLEDGE

As well as being an award-winning publisher, SPCK is the oldest Anglican mission agency in the world.

Our mission is to lead the way in creating books and resources that help everyone to make sense of faith.

Will you partner with us to put good books into the hands of prisoners, great assemblies in front of schoolchildren and reach out to people who have not yet been touched by the Christian faith?

**To donate, please visit www.spckpublishing.co.uk/donate or call our friendly fundraising team on 020 7592 3900.**

Printed and bound by CPI Group (UK) Ltd, Croydon, CR0 4YY

13/04/2025

14656472-0003